Knitting With Two Colors

dedicated to Joyce Williams

editor, Cully Swansen

book design, Meg Swansen & Amy Detjen

cover design and pre-press, JLS Photography & Graphic Design

proofreader, Tami Robus

assistant, Eleanor Haase

drawings, Meg Swansen & Elizabeth Zimmermann

photographs, Meg Swansen

photos are from garments knitted by, Kevin Ames, Janine Bajus, Amy Detjen, Ann Feitelson, Irene Katele, Betts Lampers, Dale Long, Ron Schweitzer, Meg Swansen, Marilyn van Keppel, Joyce Williams, Elizabeth Zimmermann

Schoolhouse Press

Pittsville, WI 54466

schoolhousepress.com

800-YOU-KNIT

Many of the photographed motifs are from available sweater patterns; see the list on page 63.
Nearly all techniques are demonstrated in *The Knitting Glossary DVD* with Elizabeth Zimmermann & Meg Swansen.
schoolhousepress.com

ISBN 10: 0-942018-34-6

ISBN 13: 978-0-942018-34-9

Library of Congress Control Number: 2011917681

Printed in the USA

Eco-Friendly Books
Made in the USA

Contents

Introduction	*p 4*
Getting Started	*p 5*
Garment Construction	*p 15*
Designing Your Own	*p 42*
Miscellaneous	*p 55*
Index	*p 61*
Photo Identification	*p 63*

About This Book

Many of the following techniques were included in the book we produced with Joyce Williams in 2000, *Sweaters From Camp*. We have augmented that section with many more tips and tricks, both unique and gleaned. The contents are relevant to knitting with two colors as well as most other types of knitting.

In Chapter 1 you will find the techniques and concepts to call upon before undertaking a garment.

In Chapter 2 we discuss specific techniques of garment construction in chronological order, from casting on at the lower edge of the body to knitting sleeves and finishing.

Chapter 3 contains information for designing your own garment. The ideas there are specifically for knitters who want to resize or modify an existing pattern, and those who design from scratch.

Chapter 4 contains helpful ideas that didn't fall neatly into the preceeding chapters.

Think of the varied and splendid panoply of **two-color pattern knitting** extant in the world: Turkish stockings, Latvian mittens, Icelandic yoke sweaters, Peruvian Chula caps, Swedish Bohus sweaters, Armenian garments, Norwegian Lus jackets, Estonian mittens and socks, British Fair Isle patterns, Macedonian tent socks, Faroe Islands sweater, etc.

Stranded Knitting is a generic term for two-color work, and includes most of the world's traditional color knitting. When using two colors in one round, the un-used color is carried across the back of your work as it travels to its next stitch. These strands vary in length depending how many consecutive stitches you work in one color. To minimize the lengths of the strands we employ Trapping *(p9)*.

Fair Isle Knitting is our favorite kind of color-pattern knitting. Many knitters refer to any type of color-pattern as "Fair Isle". However, true Fair Isle is a specific style of two-color knitting that originated in the Shetland Islands. It is defined by an overall design of horizontal or vertical bands of varying widths using geometric shapes. Some of the unique properties of true Fair Isle knitting are:

- both the foreground and background colors may be shaded through a motif.
- each round uses no more than two colors at a time.
- garments are worked in the round, and openings are cut where needed through use of "steeks".

The most common Fair Isle motifs are bands of "OXOs"; lozenges separated by Xs. Narrower bands, between 3 to 9 rounds high, called Peeries, separate the wider OXO bands.

If you are working a geometric Fair Isle chart, there is a soothing rhythm - a song - in each round of pattern; it is hypnotic and relaxing. On the other hand, if you knit a "picture" (as the hawk's head on page 56 or the Weeping Sun/Moon on page 41), it is exciting and intriguing with no two rounds the same.

We hope this book may help to sharpen your two-color skills so that none of the world's color-knitting traditions will be out of your reach – and that you may be inspired to become a designer.

Knit On,
Meg and Amy

Nov 2011, Cary Bluff

Chapter 1: Getting Started

Practice Two-Color Knitting

There are two reasons we recommend knitting a 2-color hat before beginning a garment.

- You can practice your two-color technique without too much concern for perfection.
- It is an accurate way to produce a swatch for a circular two-color garment.

After a Technique Practice Cap or two, you will be ready to knit a Swatch Cap for your garment.

All techniques introduced in the caps are described on the following pages.

Reading Charts

Pattern charts are read horizontally - one line at a time - from lower right to left. The pattern-repeat may be marked off (as the red box on the chart below), or only the repeat itself may be shown (below right). Sometimes the whole width of the body is charted, in which case, read the entire line from right to left, once for the front and once for the back. Then proceed to the next line up on the chart.

A Magnetic Row Finder is a useful tool; a metal sheet with a moveable magnetic strip. With a copy of the chart on the sheet, place the metal strip on the row *above* the one you are knitting. That lets you see the preceding round and double check your knitting accuracy. Highlighter Tape serves the same purpose and is more portable.

Place a marker in the first stitch of the round.

Read each chart line from right to left to the end of the repeat. Then begin again at the right hand side of the repeat, on the same line and knit that repeat over and over until you are back at your beginning marker. Move the magnetic strip, or tape, up one line and begin the next round.

Right: one full 24-stitch repeat of an OXO/Peerie pattern. Begin at lower right corner; read each line from R to L. For an average sized hat on 120 sts @ 5-1/2 sts to 1", repeat each line 5x.

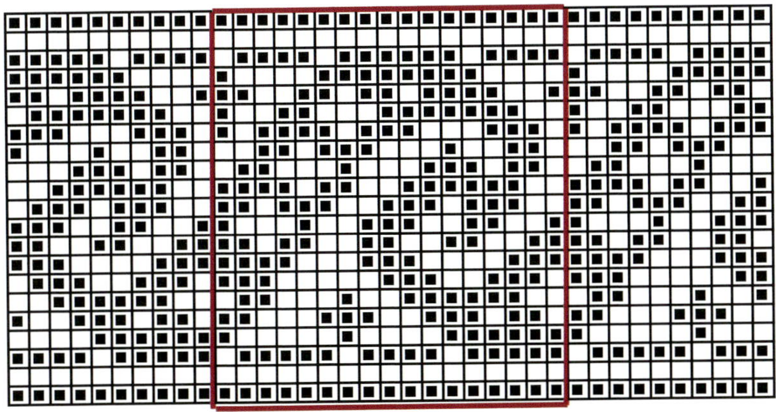

The 17-stitch repeat in the red box makes a nice cap border. Cast on 119 sts instead of 120, to fit in 7 repeats.

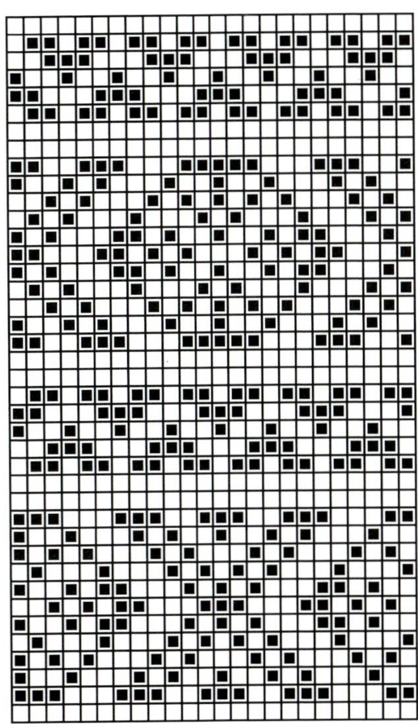

Technique Practice Cap

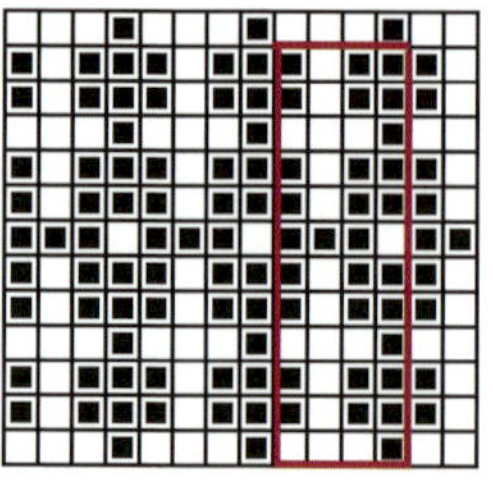

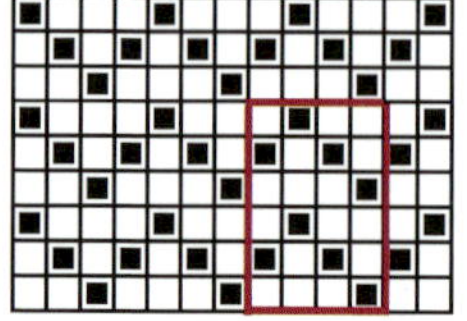

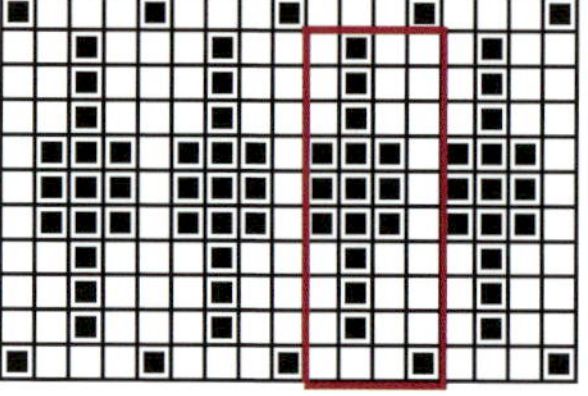

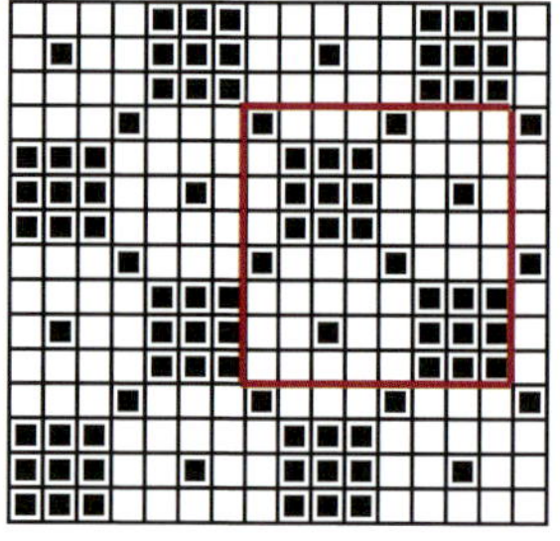

At a gauge of between 5-1/2 and 6 sts to 1", cast on 120 sts *(see Casting On, p13)*. Join for circular knitting, being careful not to twist *(p16)*.

For this small circumference, use either a 16" circular needle, or a pair of 24" needles *(p55)*.

For a rolled lower edge, knit 7 rounds of Stocking stitch (knit all stitches). Purl one round to act as a "speed bump" (see photo below) to keep the rolled edge under control.

Begin working one of the charts in the righthand column (the red box = one horizontal and vertical repeat); they all fit evenly into 120 sts. To join a second color, leave a 4-5" long tail and start knitting with the new color. The first stitch loosens as you knit, but can be tightened after a round or two. Darn in the ends later *(p20)*.

If the carried color travels over multiple stitches, make sure to carry it loosely across the back of your work. If it is too loose, it can be snugged up later; if it is too tight, the knitting will pucker and cannot be straightened.

Work about 6 inches in pattern to practice one or all of the three methods described in the next section to determine your preference.

Remember, this is just a practice piece, so experiment freely until you feel comfortable managing two strands of yarn at the same time.

Two-Color Knitting Techniques

There are basically 3 ways to handle working with 2 strands of yarn at once: both colors in your left hand, both colors in your right hand, or one color in each hand. Each method requires one of your hands to learn something new.

Whichever method you use, one yarn travels over the other to get from one place to another. Naturally, the other must

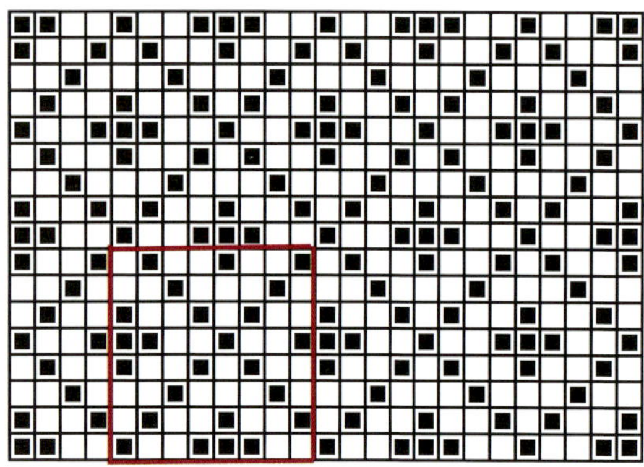

red box = one horizontal and vertical repeat

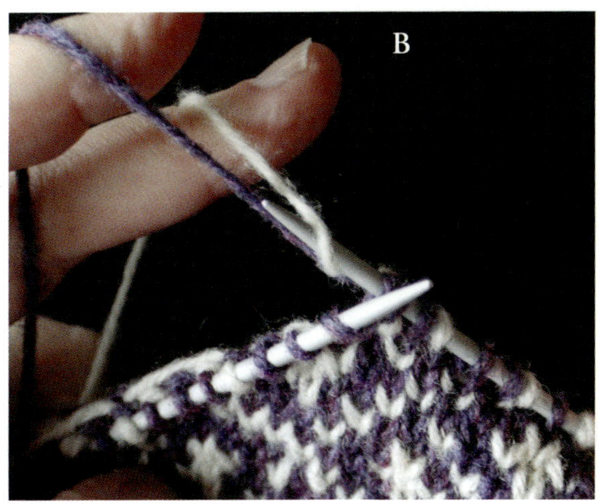

travel under. We use the terms "over" and "under" to describe the placement of the two colors; see a brief discussion of Over and Under on page 55.

One Color in Each Hand, photo A: This technique is recommended to new color knitters because you can keep a ball of wool on each side of you; no tangling. Each color is poised and ready to be worked, with no need to put down one color and pick up the other.

You may begin by doing some plain knitting with your new hand until it feels more confident. Now, using your favorite hand, add in a second color and begin following one of the charts on the opposite page. Continue on your Practice Cap.

Both Colors in Left Hand, photo B: You may hold the MC (main color) over your index finger and the CC (contrasting color) over your middle finger. As you knit with the MC, the second finger stays out of the way until needed. When knitting the CC from the second finger, you can go over (as in photo) or under the MC.

Some knitters have both strands over their left forefinger and control the tension by wrapping the working wools around other fingers.

Both Colors in Right Hand, photo C: One method is to hold one color between your right thumb and forefinger and the second color over your middle finger.

Swatch Cap

When your 2-color practice cap(s) yields a consistant fabric, you're ready to obtain an accurate gauge for your project by knitting a Swatch Cap with the wool and pattern you have chosen for your sweater.

To obtain an accurate gauge for a color-patterned circular garment, your swatch should also be color-patterned and circular, unless you are one of those rare knitters whose knit and purl stitches match each other perfectly in two-color knitting.

Using a method of your choice, cast on *(p13)* between 110 and 130 sts, depending upon your pattern. For example, if your pattern has a 24-stitch repeat, cast on 120 sts (24x5); if your pattern has a 32-stitch repeat, cast on 128 (32x4).

Join for circular knitting being careful not to twist *(p16)* and mark the first stitch of the round.

Knit 7 rounds of Stocking stitch (knit all stitches) for a rolled lower edge. Purl one round as a "speed bump" to keep the edge from rolling further *(photo on p6)*.

Begin working the chart for your project *(see Reading Charts, p5)*.

Measuring Gauge: Work at least 4 vertical inches in your chosen color pattern, put all stitches on a thread, steam block *(p41)* and take a stitch gauge reading as follows: With the cap flat on a hard surface, measure an even number of inches horizontally across the cap. Carefully count the number of stitches within those inches. Divide the number of stitches by the number of inches. For row gauge, measure at least 3" vertically and divide the number of rows by the inches.

Armed with an accurate gauge, you may now start your sweater and finish the cap later.

To finish the cap, knit until the piece is about 6 inches from lower edge, then establish 4, 5 or 6 decrease points. For example, on the 120 stitch hat with 5 dbl-dec points *(p24 for dbl-dec)*:

Round 1 (dec): (K21, dbl-dec) 5x.
Round 2: Knit.
Round 3: (K19, dbl-dec) 5x.

Continue until **half** the original number of stitches remain. Now work the decreases **every** round, down to 5 sts. Draw wool through remaining raw sts, pull firmly and darn in.

Trapping the Wools

When carrying the un-used wool across a large number of stitches, you may eliminate a long float by trapping the carried color as you knit. For instance, generally speaking, Amy traps every third stitch and Meg traps every fifth stitch, depending upon gauge.

We'll discuss trapping from the perspective of one color in each hand, and you can extrapolate the process if you hold both colors in one hand.

Trapping the Lefthand Color: As you knit along with the righthand color, you naturally hold the lefthand color out of the way. To trap the lefthand color, you must get it in the way of the stitch:

1. Insert tip of right needle into the stitch.
2. Bring the lefthand wool forward slightly, so that it rests in the V created by the 2 needles (see drawing below).
3. As you complete the stitch with the righthand color, the lefthand color will slip to the back. The arrow indicates the path of the righthand color. Notice that the lefthand color floats *over* the completed stitch.
4. Knit the next stitch with the righthand color, but do not trap the lefthand color. When you do this, the lefthand color floats *under* the completed stitch. We usually trap every 3 to 5 sts.

Trapping the Righthand Color: As you knit along with the lefthand color, you naturally hold the right-hand color out of the way. To trap the righthand color, you must get it in the way of the stitch:

1. Insert tip of right needle into the stitch.
2. Wrap the righthand color around the needle as if to knit.
3. Wrap the lefthand color around the needle as if to knit.
4. Unwrap the righthand color, back the way it came.
5. Complete the stitch with the lefthand color.

Another Method: Joyce Williams didn't want to risk the trapped color showing through on the "right" side. She would leave long strands to float across the back and catch them on the subsequent round by knitting under them every 3 or 4 sts.

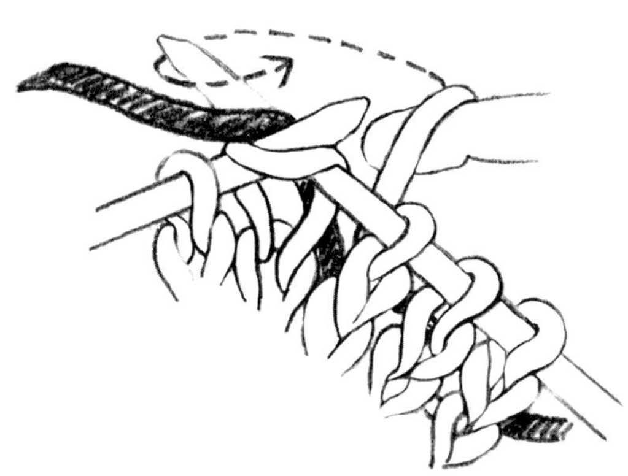

lefthand color trap

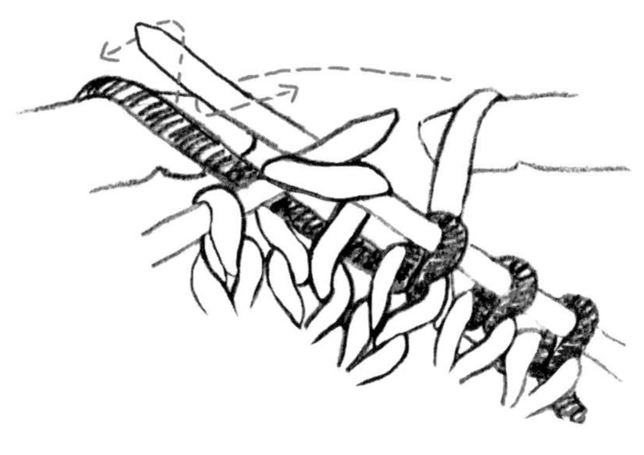

righthand color trap

The Importance of Gauge

There are many things that can affect your stitch and row gauge:

- different knitting styles (pickers vs throwers)
- different needle materials (metal vs bamboo)
- subtle needle size difference (some needle manufacturers say a US 3 is 3.0 mm - some say 3.25 mm)
- knitting back and forth vs circular knitting
- working color-patterns vs single-color
- and your mood can affect your gauge

Choosing the right needle size to obtain gauge is a very personal matter. The needle sizes given in any pattern are those used by the designer and may bear little resemblance to the size you actually use to achieve the recommended gauge.

Stitch Gauge: We cannot over-emphasize the importance of stitch gauge. Your stitches-to-the-inch may vary from the instructions, yet you can still achieve a perfectly-fitting garment; the critical point is that you know your gauge.

Shetland wool looks wonderful at any gauge from 6 st/in to 8.5 st/in. The difference between fabric knitted firmly vs. fabric knitted more loosely is the drape and density and the amount of wool used.

Since most allover color-patterned garments are knitted in the round, for the most accurate reading measure your gauge on a circular swatch. We advise knitting the Swatch Cap on page 8 or work a Speed Swatch *(p12)*. Anxious to get started on the garment, some knitters cast on a sleeve and check their gauge after about 6-8".

Row Gauge: This is often overlooked by both knitters and designers. A sleeve pattern may instruct you to increase 2 stitches every 5th round. Your stitch gauge may match the designer's perfectly, however, if your stitches are square *(p11)*, all your increases may be done before you reach the elbow and you would have had to space the increases further apart.

Some knitters get different row gauges when changing to needles made of different materials. For instance, a steel needle may yield a different gauge from an identical diameter bamboo needle. For the most part, you can ignore row gauge and knit until the garment is wanted length. However, in certain instances, such as fitting vertical repeats into a yoke, knowledge of your row gauge is vital.

A Story of Amy and Nancy: They were knitting the same color-patterned design on the same size and brand of needle - and were getting an identical stitch gauge ... to the millimeter. But when they reached 20 inches, Amy had knitted 168 rows and Nancy had knitted 145 rows: identical stitch gauges, but quite different row gauges.

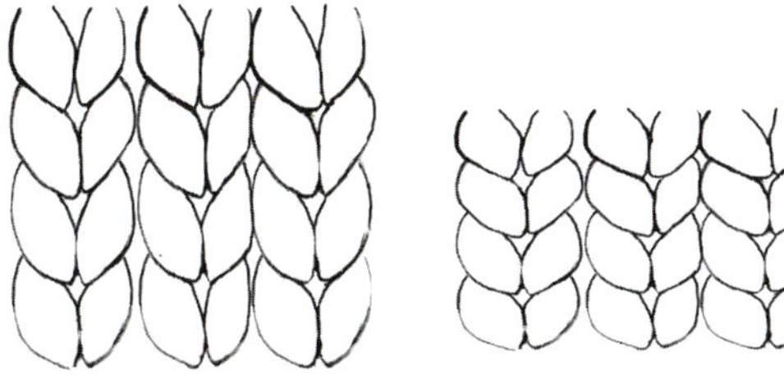

Where Nancy's stitches were rather oval (elongated), Amy's were round (squat). The result was that the same number of stitches fit in a 4 in wide swatch, but Amy knitted more rows to achieve 4 inches of height. You may occasionally get more stitches than rows to one inch! This usually happens when the pattern has a decidedly diagonal motif, but may also be the result of different knitting styles.

Frequently, you can use the already-knitted body as a giant swatch from which to take a row gauge reading.

Do you knit squat stitches like Amy? If so, you will:

- Need more than the recommended amount of yarn (more rows = more yarn).
- Increase at a different ratio from the pattern. For instance, if it says increase every 4 rounds on the sleeve, you may need to increase every 5 or 6 rounds instead.
- Need to stay alert to any ratios the pattern may call for. If it tells you to knit up 80 stitches along an edge, you may need to knit up 90 to get the same ratio they intended.

Conversely, if you knit more elongated stitches than the designer called for, you may have the opposite problems from those listed above and you may end up with leftover yarn.

This applies to picture knitting, or intarsia as well. A graph for an elephant may turn into a turtle with a trunk if your row gauge is too squat.

Speed Swatch

If you are anxious to get going on the sweater and do not want to work hundreds of stitches on a Swatch Cap, consider a Speed Swatch. This is actually a flat, circular swatch.

With a circular needle, cast on about 40 stitches and work a few ridges of garter stitch (back and forth) to prevent curling. Add the second color and *knit across the 40 stitches in pattern. Slide the stitches back around the circular needle, so that the first stitch is again at the tip of the left needle. Pull out long strands of both colors, loop them loosely across the back and repeat from *.

Continue until you have about 5 inches of fabric. Steam block the swatch *(p41)* and take a reading, staying a few stitches in from the distorted selvedges. Since you have only knitted with the "right" side facing, you have a flat, circular swatch.

Tip: Work first and last stitch of each row with both colors together to minimize selvedge distortion.

Since there is no cutting, this swatch can always be ripped out later if you need the wool. If you are fortunate enough to have your Knitting Back Backward *(p55)* gauge match your forward gauge, you can work the swatch in that manner and avoid the sloppy loops across the back.

a speed swatch in action

Resizing

Add Stitches: The most obvious solution to making a garment larger or smaller than the published design is to add to (or reduce) the number of stitches you cast on. Adjust all the subsequent numbers by the same percentage *(see EPS on p43)*.

Change Gauge: Another way to resize a garment is to work at a gauge that is looser or firmer than the gauge listed in the pattern. For example, a pattern calls for 7 stitches to an inch (or 28 stitches to 4 inches), and the 40-inch size has 280 stitches for the body. If you want a 45 inch circumference, but don't want to add stitches, you could knit at a gauge of 6.25 stitches to an inch (or 25 stitches to 4 inches).

To resize this way, take the number of stitches for the body (280) and divide it by the circumference you want (45). In this case, it came out to 6.22. Round up to the nearest quarter of an inch, and see if that is a gauge you can achieve happily.

Notice that changing from 28stitches/4 inches to 25stitches/4 inches yields *5 more inches* of circumference. This demonstrates perfectly the importance of an accurate gauge swatch.

Casting On

There are over 40 ways to cast on; here are the ones that we think pertain specifically to two-color knitting. To help prevent the lower edge from curling, especially for Corrugated ribbing *(p16)*, we recommend German Twisted or Cable cast on.

Many directions instruct you to begin with a slip knot; we prefer to have no knots in our knitting, so here is Elizabeth Zimmermann's trick to eliminate the slip knot at the start of any long-tail cast on method:

Set your hands as shown in drawing A. From behind the thumb-forefinger strand, dip the needle down (drawing B), then twist it towards yourself and point it to the ceiling. This backward loop is stitch number one, which you can see in drawing C.

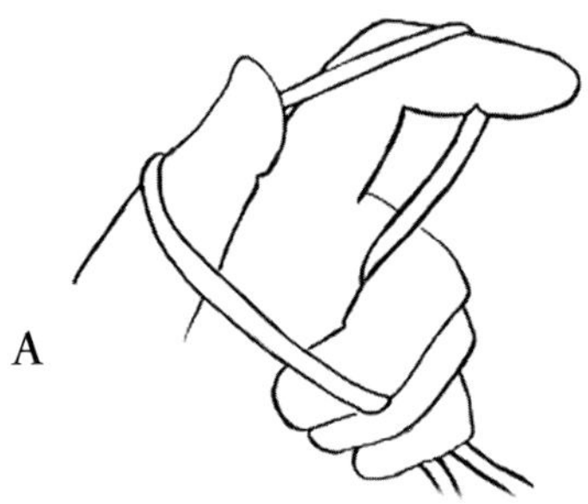

Set up for two-strand cast on with the ball strand over your thumb and tail strand on your forefinger. Tip: If, near the end, the tail length looks as if it is too short, switch the strands (the thumb strand uses less wool).

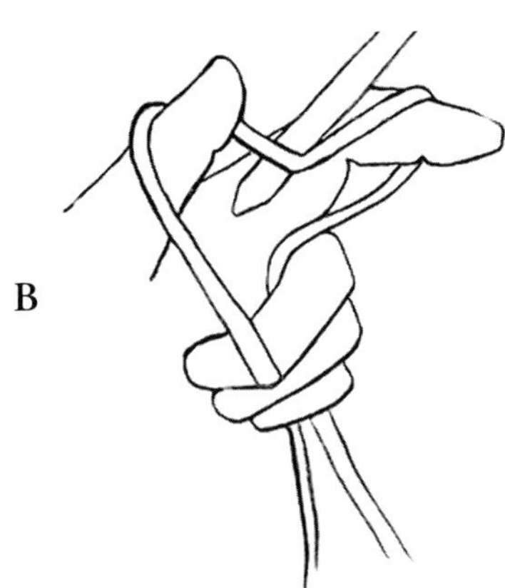

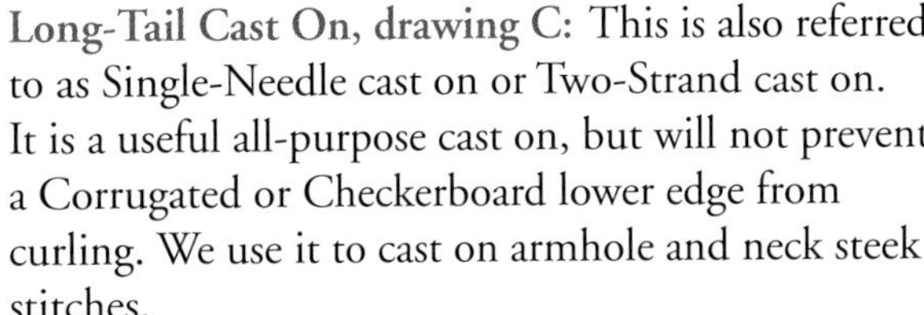

Long-Tail Cast On, drawing C: This is also referred to as Single-Needle cast on or Two-Strand cast on. It is a useful all-purpose cast on, but will not prevent a Corrugated or Checkerboard lower edge from curling. We use it to cast on armhole and neck steek stitches.

Begin as in drawings A and B. Then come up into the thumb loop, go over the near forefinger strand and hook it down through the thumb loop. Release, then reset your thumb.

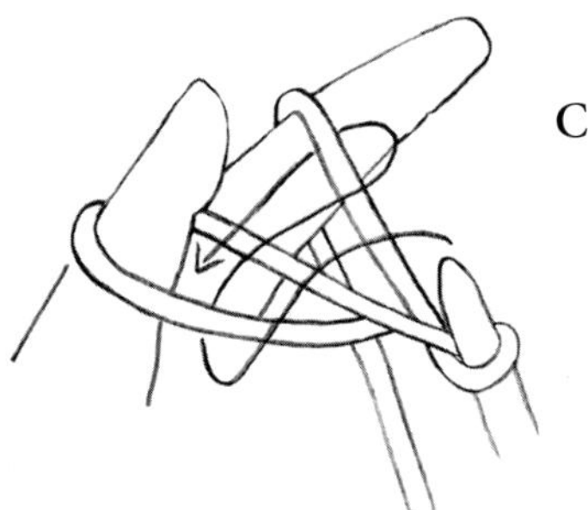

When using Long-Tail to add an underarm steek, alternate light and dark stitches as you cast on by alternating the colors over your thumb and forefinger *(photos p14)*.

German Twisted Variation, drawing D: This is also called Elastic Long-Tail and is similar to the Long-Tail cast on: Begin as in drawings A and B. Go under both thumb strands, come up over the far thumb strand and dive down into the thumb loop, then up in front of the near thumb strand. Reach over and grab the near finger strand. Now, bend your thumb slightly to enable you to get the forefinger strand into the little loop nearest the thumb. Release your thumb and reset.

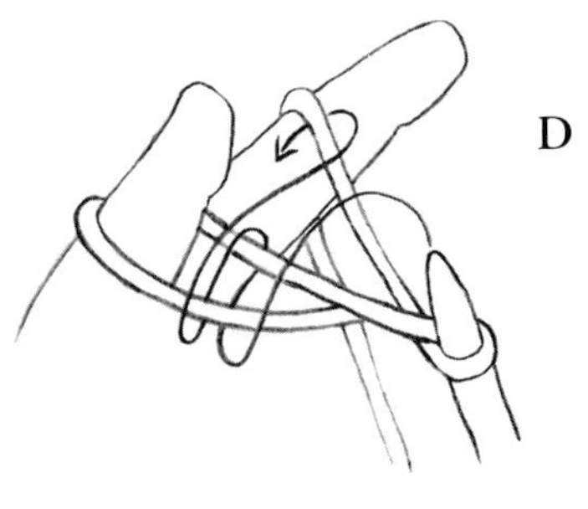

Cable Cast-On, drawing E: Nancy Robinson taught us how to avoid a slip knot at the beginning: start with the twist shown in drawings A & B, then cast on one stitch in the Long Tail method (drawing C). Switch the needle to your left hand. With a second needle, *go between the 2 stitches, hook the working wool through, put the resulting loop on left needle (twisted, or not; be consistant). Repeat from *.

To prevent the final Cable Cast-On stitch from slanting: before you place it on the left needle, bring the working wool to the front. Now put the final loop on the needle (drawing E) and take the wool to the back (from Mary Hall).

Crocheted Provisional Cast-On, drawing F: There are a number of ways to cast on provisionally, but this is our current fave. By working directly over a knitting needle you eliminate the tricky bit of trying to see which loop to knit into on the back of the crochet chain – and, we are always eager to save an extra step. With waste-wool, crochet a few chain stitches. Hold the knitting needle in your left hand and - with the crochet hook in your right hand, *reach over the top of the needle, grab the working wool and snake it through the last loop on the hook. Take the wool to the back of the needle and repeat from * (drawing F). End with a few more crochet chains, switch to the garment wool and knit on.

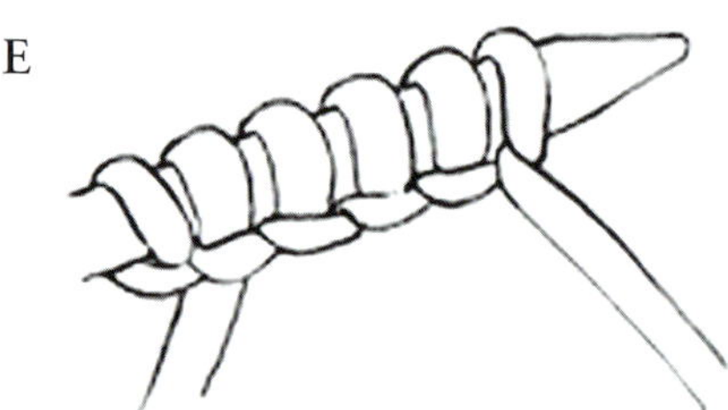

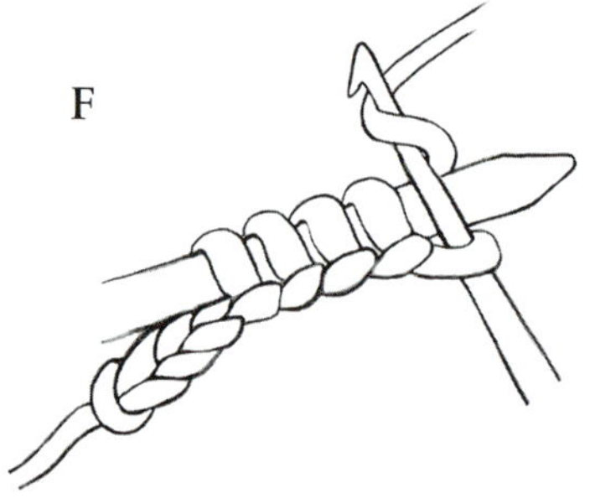

When you need those stitches again, take the end of the waste-wool and pull. The crochet chain un-zips and raw stitches are revealed.

Long-Tail casting on with two colors: Blue loop over thumb, a white stitch is cast on.

Long-Tail casting on with two colors: White loop over thumb, a blue stitch is cast on.

Chapter 2: Garment Construction

This chapter covers knitting a garment from start to finish as a step-by-step tutorial. With Gauge and Casting On covered in the preceeding chapter, the remaining steps are:

1. Establishing Circular Knitting (below)
2. Choosing Lower Borders (p16)
3. Knitting the Body (p19)
4. Shaping within Color Pattern (p21)
5. Working Armholes (p25)
6. Shaping the Neck (p26)
7. Shaping Shoulders with Short Rows (p29)
8. Securing & Cutting Steeks (p30)
9. Knitting Sleeves (p32)
10. Adding Borders & Buttonholes (p34-38)
11. Finishing (p41)

Establishing Circular Knitting

If you're knitting a pullover, cast on the required number of stitches and skip to page 16.

Plot the Center Front Steek: For a cardigan, the extra steek stitches you add at the center-front provide a field for the future cutting and are not included in the body measurement. A steek at the center front (and later at armholes and neck), permits you to work the entire body in the round.

We recommend a 7, 9 or 11 stitch wide steek, depending upon your gauge. This number includes a knit-up stitch on each side of the steek. So cast on your calculated body circumference *plus* steek stitches. Photo A below shows the steek running through the ribbing and on up the body.

Regardless of the width of the steek, only the center 3 sts are involved in the future securing-and-cutting; the remaining stitches fold back and form a facing on each side of the cut.

Striped or Speckled Steeks: Except for an occasional plain round in the chart, it is necessary to keep the steek stitches in alternate speckles (photo A), or vertical stripes (photo B). This ensures that both colors can be secured before cutting.

Knit Up Stitches flank each side of the steek. Keep these stitches in background color throughout, uninvolved in the pattern or shaping, so you easily can knit up into them when adding the borders.

A

speckled cardigan steek

B

striped cardigan steek

Join, Being Careful Not To Twist: This is a classic cry at the beginning of all instructions for circular garments. After casting on, carefully go around the needle, making sure all the knots are below the needle, with no twists. Knit into the first cast-on stitch and work the first round. Check the knots again. If you do have a twist, you can untwist it now -- between the first and last stitches -- but this is your final chance.

If you have hundreds of cast-on stitches, here is a tip for keeping them organized as you cast on: Every 20th cast on stitch, put a coilless pin over the knitting so that it hangs below the cast on edge (photo below). When you are ready to join the first to the last cast-on stitch, align all the pins to hang below the needle. Go from pin to pin to verify that the cast-on never twists over the needle. Once a segment is verified, you can slide that pin forward and scrunch up the CO edge. If the pin stays below the needle, all stitches in that segment are below the needle.

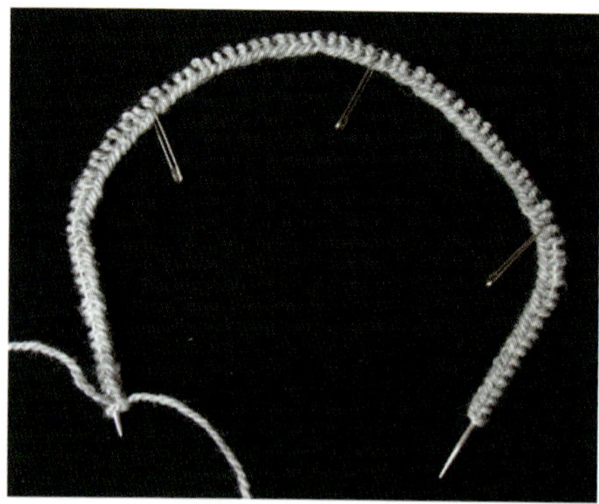

Choosing Lower Borders

Corrugated Ribbing: This is a beautiful, stable ribbing which maintains the double-thickness of an all-over patterned garment. It is achieved by working knit 2, purl 2 (or knit 1, purl 1) with two colors: knit with one color and purl with the other. You can apply color-shifting within the ribbing, in both foreground and background colors.

One method is to keep all the knit stitches in one color and shift through a series of colors in the purl section. If you purl a stitch of one color into a different color, a "blip" of the contrasting color will be brought up into the new-color round. Sometimes this is desirable, as it may help to merge two similar shades. However, if the contrast is very high, the blip can be annoying and look like the "wrong" side. In that case, you may *knit* all the purl stitches with the new color for one round only, then return to purl for subsequent rounds of that color; no wrong side blips.

If you decide to have a single color rib at the edges of an all-over patterned garment, it will feel decidedly flimsy. You can beef up that plain ribbing by working Amy's Single-Color Corrugated rib: knit 2 sts with one strand, purl 2 with another strand of the same color.

If you want all edges of a cardigan to have an uninterrupted Corrugated rib, cast on Provisionally and add

Corrugated rib, shading colors in both k and p

Amy's single-color Corrugated rib

the continuous border around the entire periphery after the sweater is finished *(p19, Just Start Knitting)*.

Alert: Corrugated ribbing has practically no elasticity; you must knit and purl with a continuous strand to produce an elastic rib. So if you want the lower edge to hug in slightly, cast on fewer stitches and perhaps use a smaller size needle as well.

Purl-When-You-Can is Meg's method to eliminate standard non-curling lower-edge treatments, such as ribbing, Garter stitch or a hem and it enables you to launch directly into the color pattern; no waiting. A relatively small smattering of purl stitches are required to produce a fabric which will lie flat. But, to avoid the "wrong-side-blips", only purl a stitch when it lies above a same-color stitch in the preceding round.

Only purl-when-you-can in either the motif color, or the background; you need not do both. Work for a minimum of 2".

Meg expanded the above to include front cardigan borders, knitted at the same time as the body. The occasional purl stitches also help prevent the borders from drooping (photo below, right).

Checkerboard Ribbing: Work as for 2/2 Corrugated rib, but shift every 4 rounds and put knits above purls and vice versa.

Checkerboard Garter Stitch, photo above, **aka** hell stitch:

Row 1(RS): *K2 pink, k2 green, repeat from *.

Row 2(WS): *Pink to front, p2 pink, pink to back, green to front, p2 green, green to back, repeat from *.

To achieve the same result in a less stressful manner, use Amy's variation and carry only one color at a time: For Row 2, pink to front, *p2 pink, slip 2 purlwise with yarn in front, repeat from *. This row works only the pink purls. Work this row a second time and purl only the green stitches; slip pinks.

Hems are another method to prevent the lower edge from curling and there are a number of different ways to work them. This also provides an opportunity to chart and knit a name, date, a secret message, or a color pattern into the hem.

Corrugated rib, shifting colors in both knit and purl.

purl-when-you-can on lower border and cardigan edge

Hem First: Cast On Provisionally and knit the hem with a lighter-weight wool to obviate bulk. At wanted depth, switch to body wool, knit one round, purl one round and continue on body. When finished, remove Provisional cast-on and skim raw stitches to inside of fabric as described in Hem Last, below.

Hem Last: Use Long-Tail Cast-On *(p13)*. Place the outline-stitch side of Long-Tail on the outside of the body and ignore the hem until the garment is finished. With lighter-weight wool, knit up stitches from behind the outline stitch (into the purl bumps; drawing opposite) and knit hem to wanted depth. Fold up hem and pin into place. Remove from the needle about 15-20 sts at a time. With a sharp sewing up needle, tack down the stitches as you skim through the inside of the body fabric then through the live stitch. This eliminates both casting-on and binding-off, and keeps the hem as elastic as the rest of the fabric. The outline-stitch side of Long-Tail cast on makes a sharp turn and eliminates the need to purl a "turning round".

For a hem last cardigan, after the garment is finished and the cardigan front has been cut open, you can

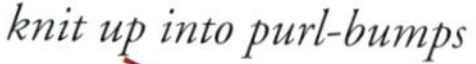

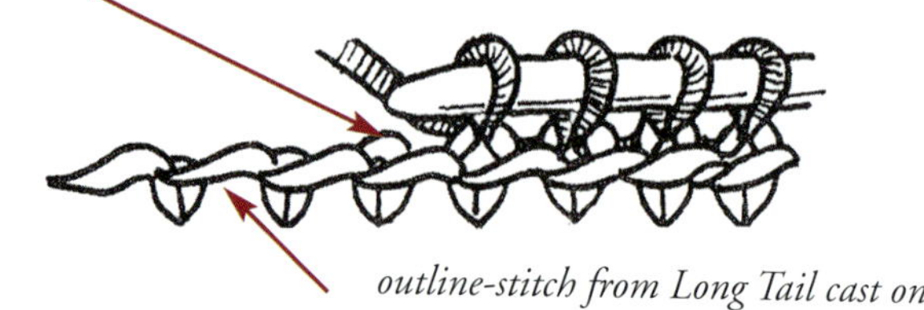

still knit the hem in the round with the use of a **Wrapped Steek:** Knit up hem stitches from behind the outline stitch as described. At center front, wrap the working wool(s) around the right hand needle 6 to 8 times (photo below); continue around. Next round: unwrap the last wraps and wrap anew. This produces a series of ladders and sloppy selvedge stitches. When hem is deep enough, snug up each selvedge stitch, cut down the middle of the ladders, fold the hem into place, skim the raw stitches to the inside of the fabric and stick the steek ends into the hem tube. The tube will be sealed off by whatever border you add.

A slightly tidier way to achieve the above result is to work a knitted steek. When done, ravel the steek stitches to produce ladders and proceed as above.

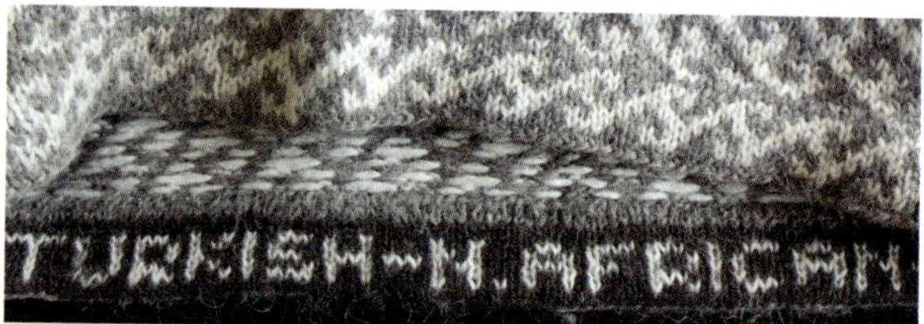

Hems can have messages knitted in, or remain speechless.

wrapped steek in progress on a hem

Just Start Knitting: Sometimes you are unsure about the final wanted length of the finished garment - or are having a difficult time deciding upon the lower edge treatment. In that case, use Provisional cast-on (make sure the first round is a plain round to ensure a clean pickup), and finish the lower edge at the end. You can adjust its depth to achieve desired length.

Knitting the Body

Balancing Color Patterns on Body: If you are resizing a garment or if you want to add some waist shaping, establish a Pivot Stitch, or panel at each underarm seam. There are examples of Pivot Stitches and a guide to balancing the color pattern in Chapter 3: Designing Your Own, plus a chart for waist shaping on page 51.

Spacing Increases Above the Ribbing: When instructions blithely say, "Increase 27 stitches evenly spaced around" we can smile and whip out Cheryl Brunette's More-or-Less Right Formula, from her book, *Sweater 101.*

Let us say you have 132 stitches on the needle and you need to increase 9 stitches evenly-spaced around. Divide 132 by 9 = 14 (ignore the remainder for the moment). To that answer, add 1 = 15.

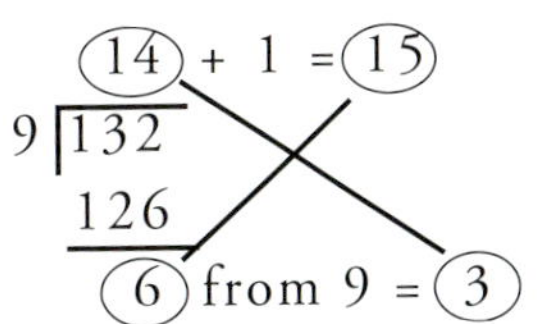

Now subtract the remainder (6) from the divisor (9) = 3. Draw a giant X as shown in the illustration and read the answer as follows: (knit 14, make one) 3 times; then (knit 15, make one) 6 times. If you are particularly finicky, you may alternate every 14th and 15th until you run out of fourteenths.

This formula also works for Decreasing evenly spaced. Use the same formula and read the answer as follows:

Turn 14 sts into 13 (k12, k2tog) 3 times; then turn 15 sts into 14 (k13, k2tog) 6 times.

Joining New Colors: Many color pattern garments call for a number of different shades of wool. As you add in each new color, you have the option to leave a long tail to be darned in later, or to splice the new color to the old.

Color changes are done at the beginning of the round; at the side seam for a pullover, or at the center front for a cardigan.

Jogless Darning In: When beginning a new color, leave a 4 to 5" tail. When you go back to darn in the ends, you can overcome the inevitable "jog" at the beginning of the round with the following tip:

As you look at the outside of the sweater, gently pull the strand-to-be-darned-in up, down, left and right. One of those directions will be the obvious choice to make it match most closely to its sister stitches.

Generally speaking, the old tail is darned up and to the right; the new tail goes down and to the left. With a sharp sewing-up needle, skim the tail through the inside of the fabric in a diagonal line. Because Shetland wool tends to felt as it is being worked, you needn't skim back into the same strand to lock it in place. It is amazing how invisible you can make the jog if you are patient.

Spit Splice to Join New Colors: Make sure the old and new ends are broken, not cut (a tufted end splices more securely). Un-twist the last 3-4" of each end. Break off one ply from each strand and overlap the two ends in your palm. Moisten your other palm and rub your hands together briskly for 5-10 seconds ... until you feel heat. The wool fibers fuse to each other and you can knit on with no discernable thickening in the wool. We usually give the spliced area a few extra twists before knitting it.

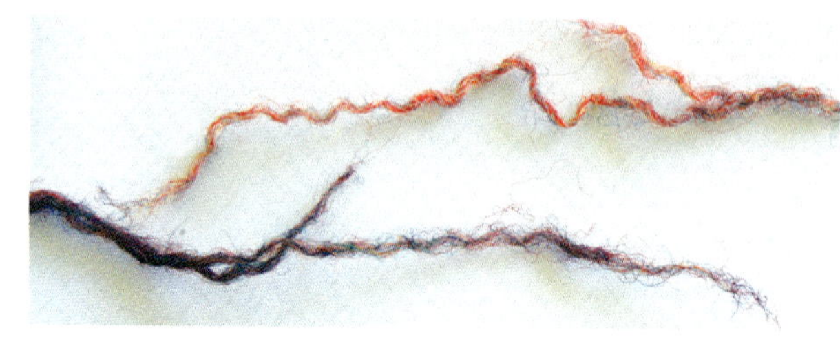

This works magically if the old and new colors are similar in tone, but even contrasting colors work if you don't mind three or four stitches of barber-pole; in a complex pattern, this will not be noticeable. The benefit is that when you are finished with the sweater, often you have only the cast on and the bound off end to darn in.

Solid Color Rounds: In traditional Fair Isle patterns, you may come across solid-color horizontal lines. Since this round has no strands across the back, it has a slightly different (wussy) feel. Amy solved this problem: Knit that row using two balls of the same color, k2 sts with one strand, k2 sts with the other strand.

A solid color round is an opportunity to insert a Short Row, see pages 27-28 for 3 different methods.

Although the colors change about every 7 rounds, only the cast-on and the cast-off ends needed to be darned in; all color joins were spliced (p-w-y-c lower border, see p17).

note the solid color rounds between OXOs

Shaping Within Color Pattern

Another beautiful feature of knitting in the round is the ability to shape within the fabric: waist shaping; bust darts; curved armholes, tapered sleeves, etc.

When working in two colors, study your knitting to see which color will be best to use for the increases. You might decide always to increase either in the background color, or in pattern color. There are so many variables and no general rule. Knitter's Choice.

Increases

M1 = Make one, or Backward Loop, or E-Wrap: With one of the working wools, make a twisted loop over the right needle. If you are working pairs of increases, you may turn each loop in an opposite direction for a mirror-image. In the drawing, the loop on the left sits backward on the needle and will be worked into the back next time it is met.

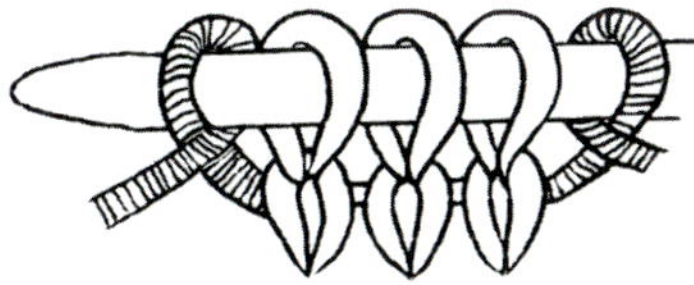

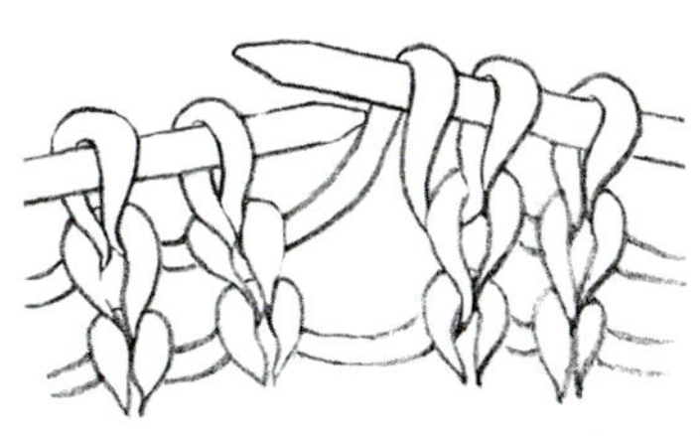

Lifted Increase *(aka Raised Running Thread Increase)*, Leans to the Left: Find the strand that connects the stitches on the right and the left needles. With the tip of the ***right*** needle, from behind, lift that strand. Insert the tip of the left needle into the front (right side of the loop) and knit.

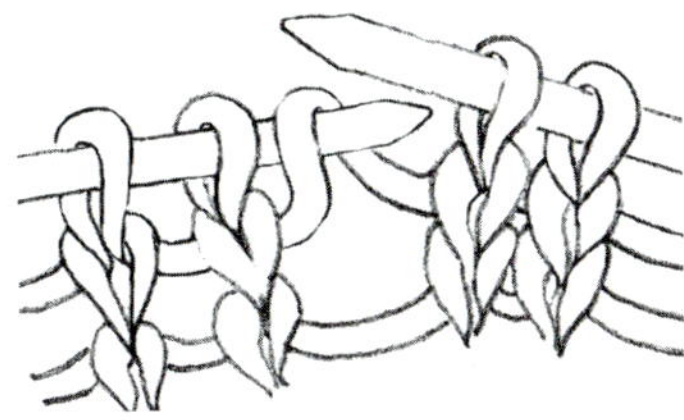

Lifted Increase, Leans to the Right: Lift the strand (from the back) with the tip of the ***left*** needle and knit into the front (left side of the loop).

The two Lifted Increases above are tantamount to working a M1 in the preceding round. Because these methods cause you to "borrow" wool from the neighboring stitches, they are snugger and less visible.

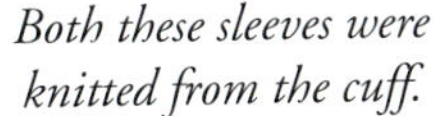

Both these sleeves were knitted from the cuff.

L: Increases are worked in background color, each side of dark, light, dark center underarm stripes.

R: Increases are worked in the next pattern color, each side of dark, light, dark center underarm stripes.

Knit Into the Back of the Stitch of the Row Below: A nearly invisible increase. Insert tip of right needle, from behind, into back of righthand side of stitch in row below. Give it a yank, leave it on the *right* needle and knit into the front with *left* needle. Now knit the parent stitch.

If you want mirror-imaged increases each side of 3 center sts: Work the above inc, k3, then with left needle, pick up the left side of the stitch in the row below (the paler shaded part in the drawing below) and knit into the front of it. It is a good idea to visually lock onto the strand in question before you knit the third stitch, as it will move down a row when the third stitch is knitted.

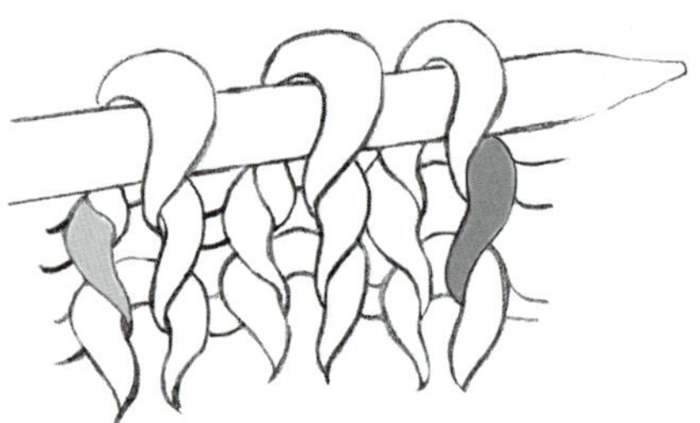

Decide whether to increase using the color of the next stitch within the motif, or always to increase using the background color and incorporate the increased stitch into the pattern on the subsequent round.

Decreases

A single decrease turns two stitches into one stitch; it must lean either to the left or to the right.

Knit 2 Together (k2tog): A single, right-leaning decrease. The second stitch on the left needle consumes the first stitch and, in a series, forms a smooth right leaning diagonal line.

Slip, Slip, Knit (ssk): A single, left-leaning decrease. Slip two stitches (one at a time) as if to knit. Insert the left needle into them and knit them together. (Invented by Barbara G. Walker and originally published in, *Knitting From the Top*.)

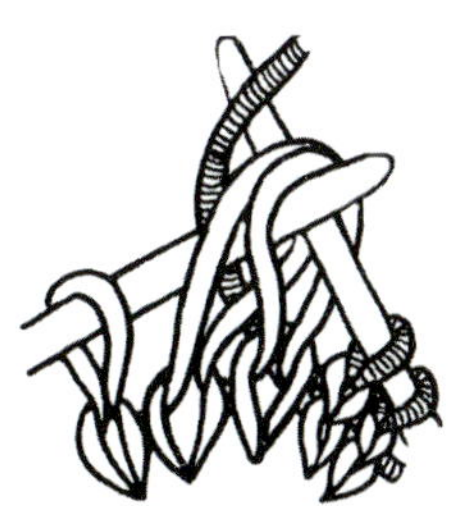

Two Alternate Methods of ssk:

1. Slip the first stitch knitwise, slip the second stitch purlwise. Insert the left needle into them and knit them together (from Dee Barrington). For us, this method results in a smoother left-leaning line.

2. Go into first stitch as if to knit. Do not remove it from needle and go into back of second stitch from right to left, k2tog. This method proves to be faster, but, for us, results in a bit of distortion.

Paired Single Decreases: You may decrease on each side of 1 or 3 center stitches. It looks very handsome if you utilize k2tog and ssk, and mirror-image them on each side.

There is no rule; you are the one to decide which look you prefer: k2tog on the righthand side, followed by ssk on the left; or the reverse.

When decreasing in two-colors, you must sometimes lean in the "wrong" direction in order for the proper color to dominate. For instance, if the next 2 sts on the left needle are light then dark and you want the resulting decrease to show as light, work ssk so the light will swallow the dark. If, however, you want the dark to be dominant, k2tog so the dark swallows the light.

pairs of single dec (k2tog, k1, ssk)

Centered Dbl Dec (CDD)

Centered Double Decrease (CDD): Instead of pairs of single-decreases *(p23)*, you can eliminate two stitches at once, by means of a Double-Decrease. There are many ways to achieve this - here is our fave:

Slip2tog knitwise, knit 1, p2sso (pass the 2 slipped sts over). The middle stitch ends up on top and the first and 3rd stitches are tucked behind it on either side.

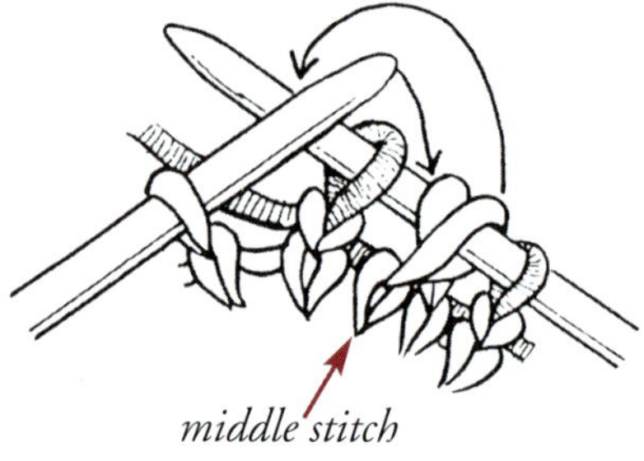

Variation on Our Favorite CDD (for speed): Slip2tog knitwise, slip 1 (knitwise or purlwise, your choice), insert the left needle into the front of all three stitches (from left to right), k3tog. See page 23 for a photo of the CDD.

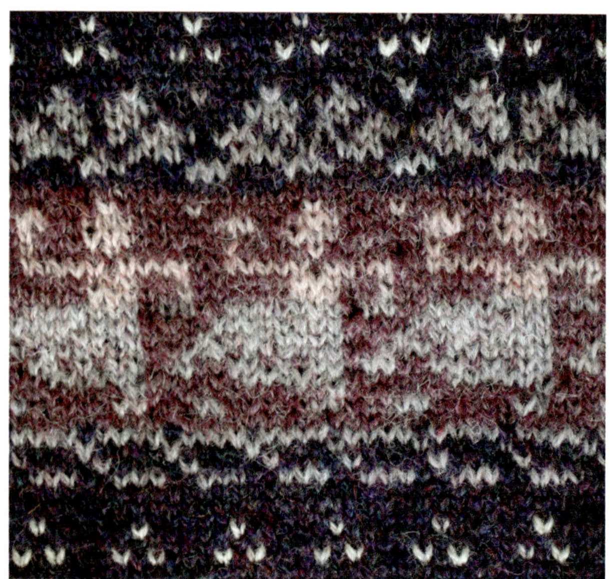

Working Armholes

Kangaroo Pouch: Work your way to wanted length to underarm. There, put underarm stitches onto a piece of wool - the number of stitches is dependant upon the depth you want the armhole set into the body. Cast on replacement steek stitches in two colors in their place *(photos on page 14)* and continue around; the result is a Kangaroo Pouch (EZ's term) that juts out at the sides.

Kangaroo Pouch

Shaping armholes in the round is a thing of beauty. In the Kangaroo Pouch photo, you can see the beginning of a curved armhole next to the speckled steek stitches.

For a curved armhole, put fewer stitches on a thread and decrease away the remaining stitches as you work around. Do not involve the future knit-up-stitches (each side of the steek) in the shaping. Every decrease round, work the following: K2tog, knit steek, ssk.

For a square armhole, put the full wanted width of the opening on a thread and work straight to shoulder.

To work the sleeve down from an inset armhole, decrease each side of the underarm for a half-gusset on the sleeve as shown below.

Bottom right photo shows Corrugated ribbing along a shaped armhole; border stitches were knitted into the Knit Up Stitch thoughtfully provided in advance. See page 52 for the decrease rate for shaping vest armholes.

half-gusset coming off a square armhole

Shaping the Neck

Kangaroo Pouches *(p25)* are also used at the base of a scooped or crew neck; a V-Neck will have only 1 or 3 sts on hold at the apex.

1

V-Neck Pullover: Put 1 or 3 center front sts onto a coilless pin (mini Kangaroo Pouch). Cast on neck steek in alternate colors and begin shaping.

V-Neck Cardigan, photo 1: You need not make a new steek, just dec each side of the existing steek at the beginning of the V, and choose the angle by the frequency of the decreases *(p53)*.

2

Wide, Shallow Neck, photo 5: A few inches shy of shoulder height, put slightly less than full wanted width of neck stitches onto a holding thread and cast on steek stitches in their place. Continue around, decreasing each side of steek to round the corners and to achieve full wanted neck width. The wide crew neck shown is bordered with black Applied I-Cord *(p35)*. Then, to prevent it from curling, Meg's "speed bump"*(p35)* is added in red.

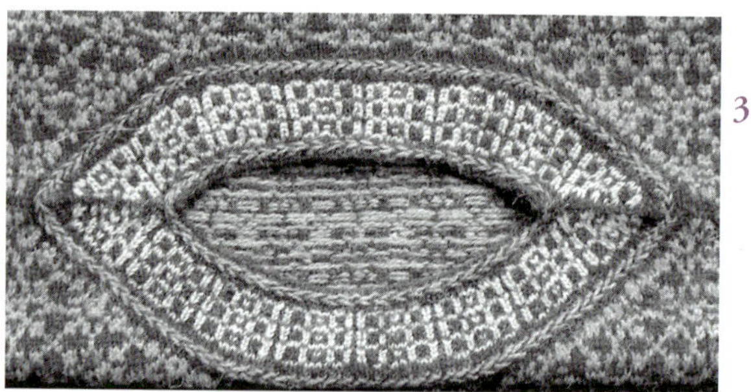
3

Scooped Neck Cardigan, photo 2: Put about half wanted neck-width stitches on a thread, cast on a steek and dec away the rest of wanted width each side of the steek.

Oval Neck, photo 3: After shaping both front and back, work border with a CDD *(p24)* at each shoulder corner, every round.

4

Square Neck (almost), photo 4: Put nearly the full wanted width of stitches onto a holding thread, cast on a steek and dec only a few stitches on each side as you work to shoulder height. When working border, miter each front corner with a CDD.

Please note: The key to the success of the Square Neck (almost) and the Oval Neck is to center the border pattern at the corners during the first round, so that the CDD uniformly consumes stitches evenly on each side. From then on, a mirror-image is automatic.

5

Short Rows

Short Rows are incomplete rows or rounds used to shape a garment. For instance, you may want to lengthen the back of the body, or add a sleeve-cap, or slope the shoulders, or add bust-darts, etc. Be aware that Short Rows within color pattern may disrupt the motifs.

Body Short Rows: If you have a single-color round between motifs, a full set of short rows would make the stripe too thick, so you can sneak in *half* short rows across the back of the body as follows: A few stitches before the side seam, turn (or Knit Back Backwards, see page 55) and work back to the same place on the other side. Break the wool, slide the stitches just worked back onto the right needle and continue around.

There are 3 Short Row methods that we recommend:

Walker's Short Rows & Wrapping, A - G

Knit Side:

1. At the turning point, slip next stitch purlwise to right needle (**A**).
2. Bring wool to front, between the needles.
3. Replace slipped stitch to left needle (**B**).
4. Turn, bring wool forward (see the working wool wrapped around the base of the slipped stitch (**C**)), and purl to next turning point. (Alternate 4: Do not turn, but Knit Back Backwards, see p55.)

Purl Side:

1. At turning point, leave wool in front and slip next stitch purlwise to right needle.
2. Take wool to the back (between the needles).
3. Replace slipped stitch to left needle.
4. Turn. Take wool to back and knit to first "wrap".

Invisible Part, Knit Side: With slipped-and-wrapped stitch on left needle (**D**), put tip of right needle under wrap and into slipped stitch and knit the two strands together (**E**).

Invisible Part, Purl Side: With slipped-and-wrapped stitch on left needle, use tip of right needle to lift the horizontal bar of the wrap on the knit side (side away from you) onto left needle (**F**), p2tog (**G**).

Yarn-Over Method, H - N

Knit Side: At the turning point, simply turn. Wrap the working wool over right needle (yarn over), from front to back (**H**). Bring wool forward and purl to next turning point.

Purl Side: At turning point, simply turn. Wrap wool around right needle from back to front to back (**I**) and knit to the yo that was worked on the knit side.

Invisible Part, Knit Side: Work yo together with **next** stitch on left needle using k2tog (**J** and **K**).

Invisible Part, Purl Side: Purl to yo. With wool in back, slip yo to right needle (**L**). Slip next stitch knitwise to right needle. Replace both stitches to left needle (**M**) and, wool forward, p2tog through back loops (tbl) (**N**).

Japanese Method, O - R

Knit Side: At the turning point, simply turn. Place a marker over the working wool (we like a coilless pin; the hook-on markers sometimes come unhooked) and snug it up against the knitting (**O**).

Purl Side: Purl to next turning point, turn. Place another marker over the working wool and snug it up against the knitting (**P**).

Invisible Part, Knit Side: Knit to first turn; tug on the pin (**Q**) and pick up that strand onto the left needle; k2tog (the pulled strand and the following stitch on left needle).

Invisible Part, Purl Side: Purl to next turn; tug on the pin (**R**), slip that strand to right needle, slip next stitch knitwise to right needle, replace both strands to left needle and p2tog tbl (same as **N**). Onward.

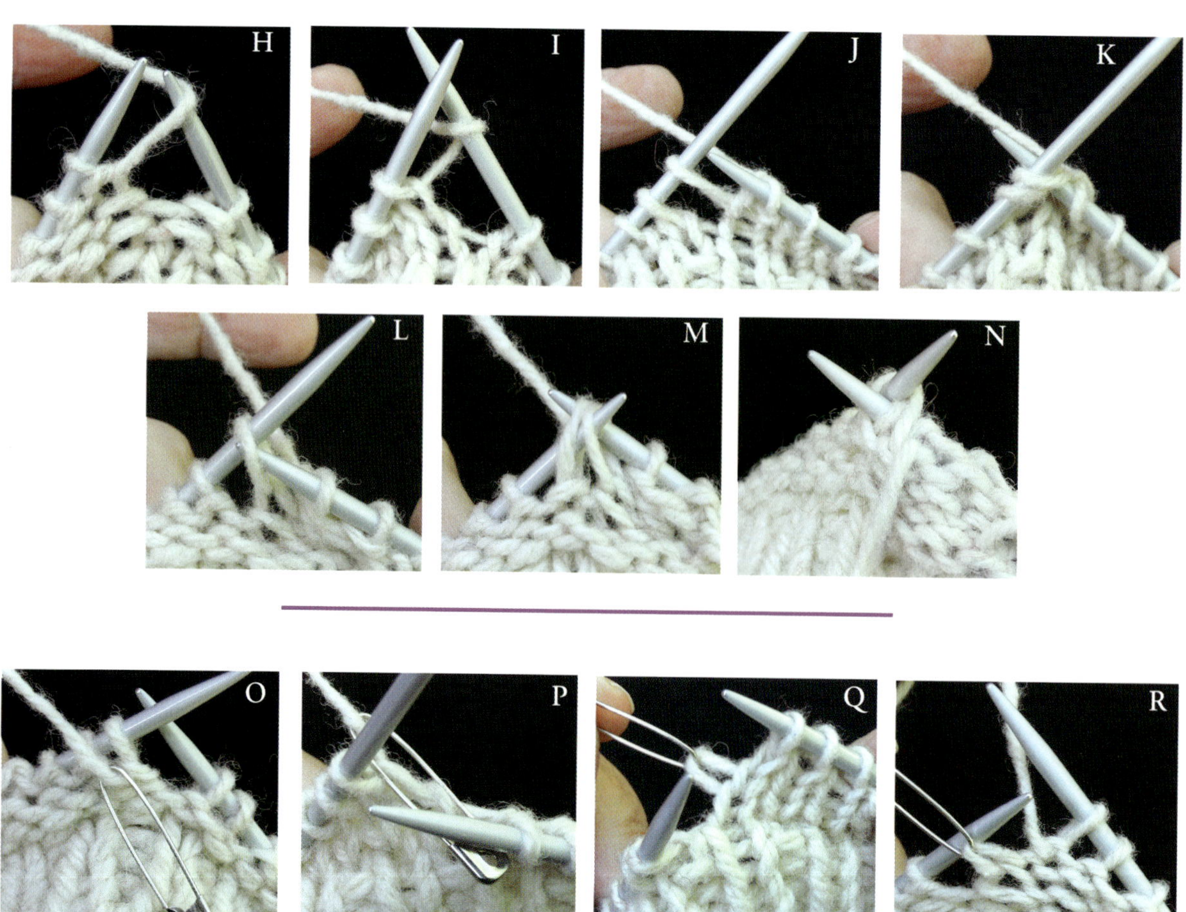

Shaping Shoulders with Short Rows

A relatively new method was discovered by Joyce Williams: Work short rows across the front only, 3 to 5 sts less each row, until you have the depth and slope you want for the shoulders. In other words, knit across front to within x-sts of the armhole. *Wrap, turn and work back (right through the neck steek) to x-sts from other armhole. Repeat from *, shortening the rows in x-stitch increments.

The number of short row sets you work depends upon your gauge and the slope you want for the shoulder.

Now unite the shoulders and note that the neck back has automatically been lowered; an added bonus.

In the photo below, the short rows are worked in solid background color, rather than have a mis-matched motif across the shoulders.

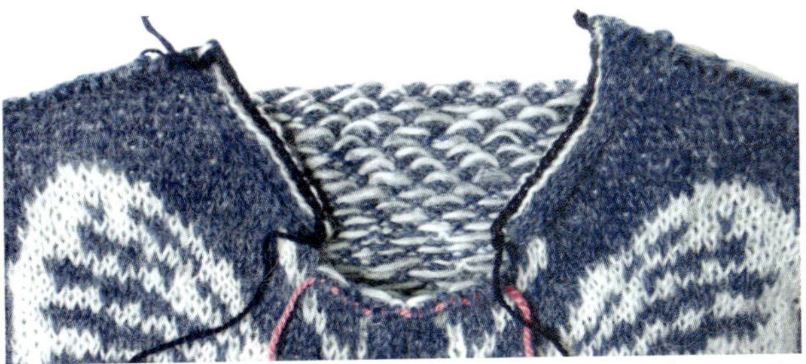

Joyce's short rows across front only (Armenian knitting)

Janine's photo of Short Rows in the Round

Short Rows in the Round

Another new technique was telepathically developed simultaneously by Janine Bajus and Mabel Corlett. The advantage is that the motif matches perfectly - in a sloping manner - fore and aft.

Janine calls this ***Short Rows in the Round*** and we have her kind permission to give you a description (more from Janine at *feralknitter.com*).

With armhole steek stitches on threads, *work in color pattern to within x-sts of the armhole. Put those x-sts (as it might be, 3 to 5 sts) on a thread PLUS the same number of stitches on the other side of the armhole. Knit the next available stitch (the one just after stitches on a thread) and snug it up against its neighbor. Continue following the chart to within x-sts of the other armhole. Repeat as above and one *Short Row in the Round* is done. Repeat from *, working to within x-sts of the holding thread and placing the unused stitches on the thread as many times as needed.

To unite shoulders and tidy the seam at the same time (below left), work 3-Needle I-Cord cast off, or 3-Needle cast off *(p39)*. There. Is that not a thing of beauty?

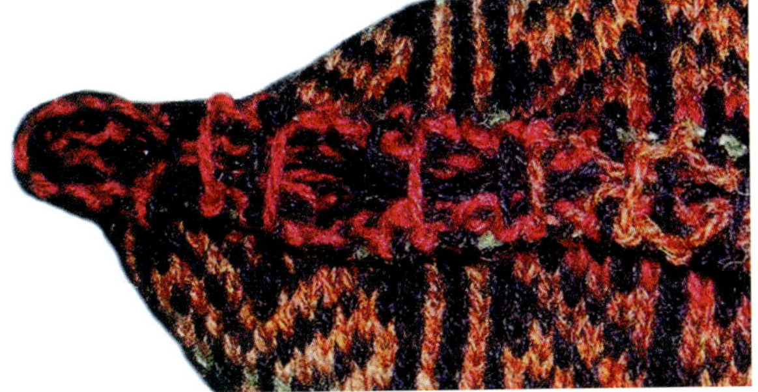

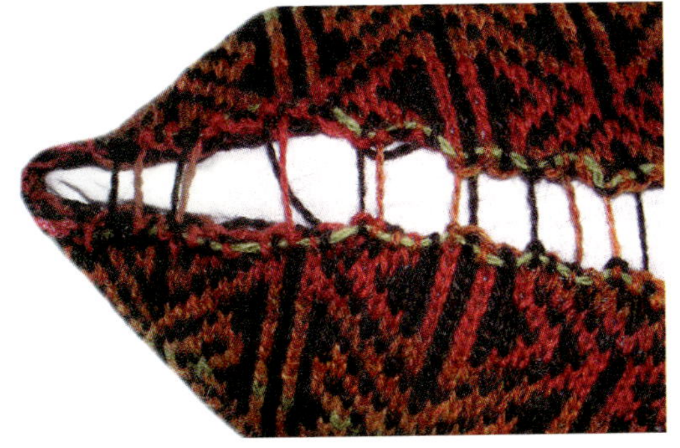

*Janine's photos, **above**: shaped shoulder just knitted; **below**, stretched apart so you can see what was done.*

Securing & Cutting Steeks

There are several ways to prepare steek stitches before cutting.

Crochet Method: No matter how many steek stitches you have, only the center three are directly involved in this procedure. Think of them as six halves and mentally number them as in the drawing below.

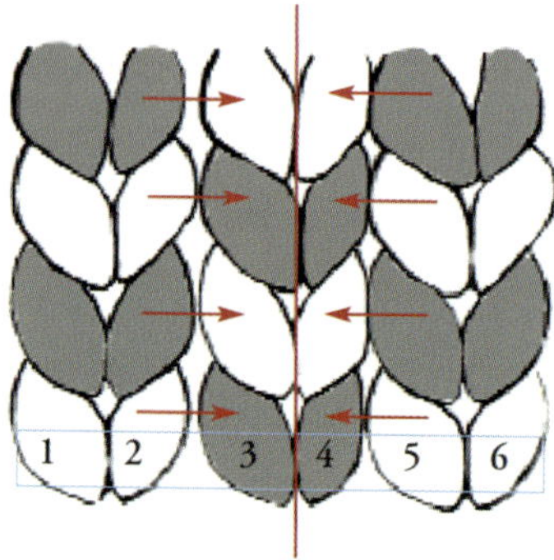

Start at the lower edge - see starting tip, below right - and chain together *(thank you, Amy Detjen)* the right half of one stitch with the left half of its neighbor (#2 and 3) all the way to the top of the steek. Chain down the other side of the center stitch, uniting the left half of its neighbor to right half of the center stitch (#4 and 5).

Whether you have striped or speckled steeks, always combine a half light stitch with a half dark stitch, so both colors are secured with each chain.

From bottom to top; go through one strand each of light and dark with each chain (#2 and 3 on the drawing). We find it easier to turn the garment sideways and work from R to L.

... and down the other side uniting strands #4 and 5.

When finished, cut through both colors of horizontal bars between the two halves of the center stitch (#3 - 4). Armholes: Snip up to the horseshoe crochet *(see Armhole Steek Tip, p31)*.
Cardigan: Cut straight through the top.

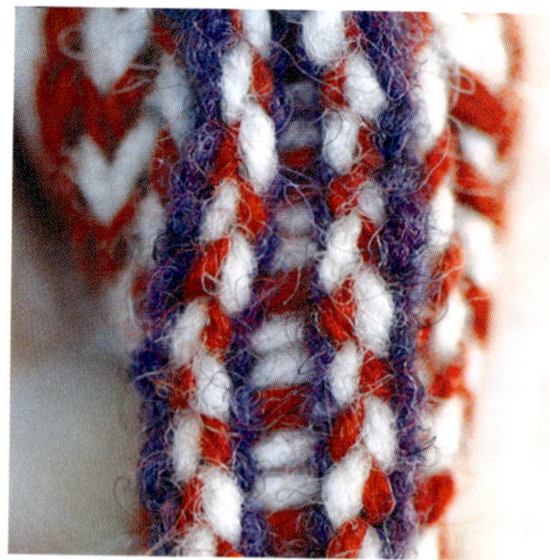

Ready to cut the horizontal bars connecting each stitch. Do not snip through any part of the crochet..

Starting Tip: The only difficulty we have had with the crocheted steek was at the beginning and the ending of the crocheted lines. Janine Bajus enlightened us with her method for additional security: Begin to crochet at the left edge of the steek (where it joins the body) and motor along the cast-on edge to the center of the steek. Make sure to capture both colors of the cast-on with each chain stitch. Continue up the steek and down the other side as described above; chain your way out to the far side of the steek.

Armhole Steek Tip: Before securing an armhole steek, we recommend weaving the raw steek stitches to each other. You have 7 or 9 raw steek stitches on your needle; weave together the left half of the steek stitches to the right half. A rudimentary weave of 3 sts to 4 won't be pretty, but it will form a horseshoe. Now you can make a tidy armhole by crocheting right through the weave.

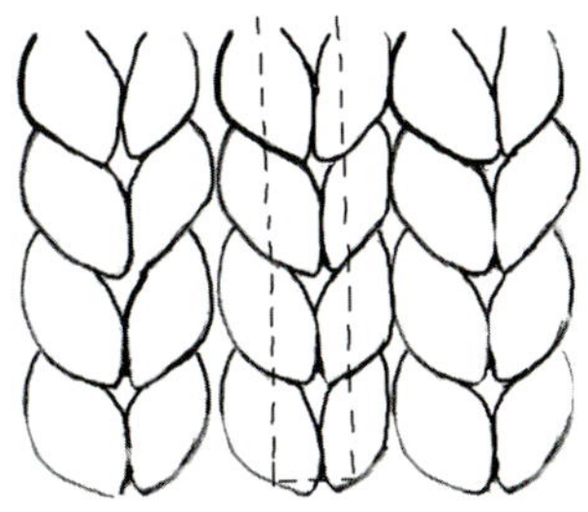

Sewing Machine Method: This variation is sometimes referred to as the Norwegian or Scandinavian method. With a length of contrasting color wool, baste down the middle of the center steek stitch. On your sewing machine, select a small stitch and a loose tension, machine stitch down one side of the basting, across the bottom and up the other side. If you can, keep the stitching in the L and R halves of the center stitch *(drawing, right)*; it makes a very tidy edge with no tufts to deal with after cutting.

Depending upon your degree of paranoia, you may repeat this operation and provide the security of a second row of machine stitching right next to – or on top of – the first line. Remove the basting wool and cut between the 2 halves of the center stitch.

Cardigan Tip: If you haven't spliced in each new color *(see Joining New Colors on p19)* the center front steek will have ends: comb them with your fingers so they lie perpendicularly to the steek. The machine stitching will nail down the strands. Then you can snip them off and eliminate the necessity of darning in ends.

Do Nothing: If you are using pure 100% Shetland Wool you may simply cut the steek open with no advance preparation. The fleece from Shetland sheep has an inherent propensity to felt ... sometimes you can actually see and feel it happening as you knit. Because of this, the surface hairs become entangled with each other to the point that the knitted fabric is reluctant to rip. Both Sheila McGregor and Michael Pearson mention this method of steeking in their books. You might feel more confident securing the stitches first.

Finishing: The remaining steek is folded back to form a facing. Then tuck under only the half stitch with machine stitches in it and tack down with thread for a beautiful result.

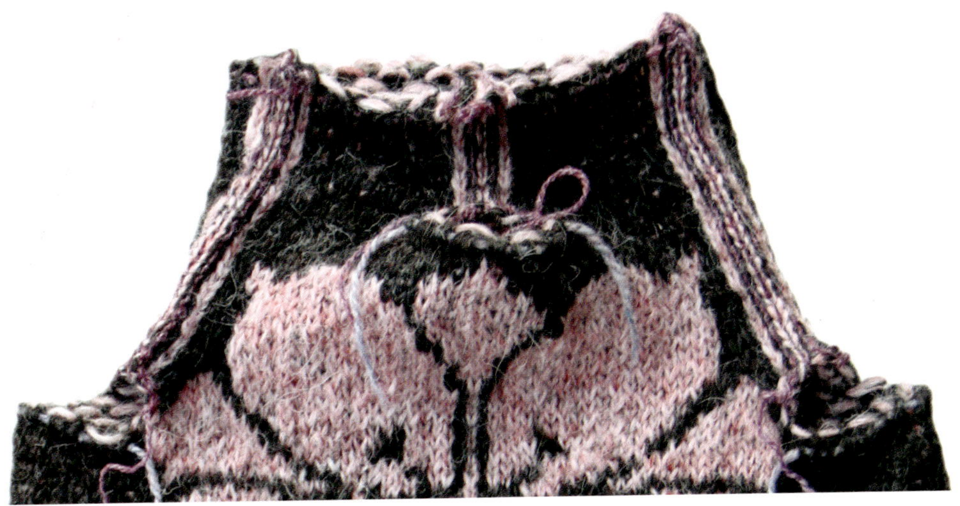

Armholes and neck front steeked and ready to cut. Isolated motif; an example of Armenian knitting.

Knitting the Sleeves

From the top or from the cuff?

Sleeves from the Top

Knitting Up Around the Armhole: Pick up underarm stitches from their thread, then find the vertical knit-up stitch. Decide which part of it you will knit-up into: the right side, the left side, both sides, the horizontal bar between the sides, or our fave - hook up the working wool from between the 2 halves of the knit-up stitch; no distortion and the snuggest connection to the fabric.

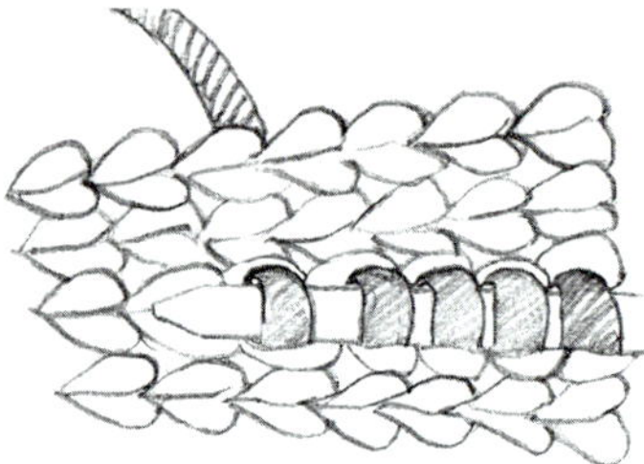

Note: There is an inevitable gap at each side of the horizontal stitches-on-a-thread and the vertical knit-up stitches. When you reach that gap, find the sloppiest thread, twist it, put it on the left needle and k2tog - or ssk, whichever looks best.

Knitting Up in Color Pattern: If knitting a diagonal color pattern, which causes stitches and rows to be more square to each other, you can produce the illusion of a continuous motif from cuff to cuff, even though the sleeves are knitted perpendicularly to the body *(4 examples on p46)*. In this case, step back one more vertical stitch from the steek and knit up between the two stitches in 2-colors, duplicating the pattern ahead of you *(photos below)*.

Ratio of Picked-Up Stitches to Rows: A good question, and one to which there is no definitive answer. Some empirical testing is required; see Amy & Nancy on page 11. When knitting up around an armhole to work a sleeve down from the top, try knitting up 3 sts for every 4 rows (knit up into rows 1, 2 and 3, skip 4; into 5, 6 and 7, skip 8, etc); or 4:5, 5:6, 6:7 or even 7:8.

When adding a Garter stitch border to a Stocking stitch sweater, EZ determined that if you knit up 2 sts for every 3 rounds, square Garter stitch will lie flat next to perpendicular Stocking stitch. Once again, experiment with your stitch-to-row ratio.

Keeping Track of Inc and Dec: When counting rows between increases or decreases, a String Thing is useful: Double a piece of string and tie a knot just below the fold-over-loop. Tie another knot just below the first knot, leaving enough space to slip the needle between the knots. To inc every 6 rounds, tie 6 knots, etc. Begin with the needle through the loop. Each time you come to the marker, move it down one knot. When you get to the bottom, it is time to increase or decrease, then move the top loop back over the needle.

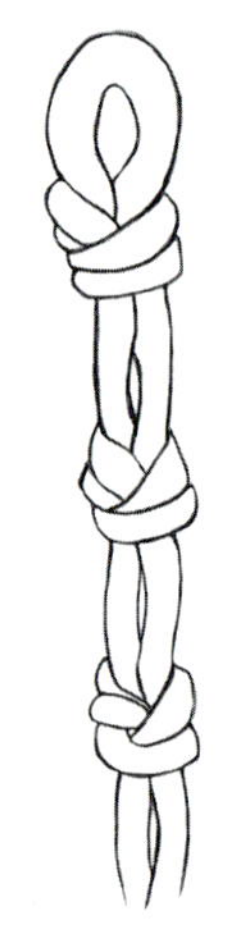

Shaping Down Sleeve Top: This is Meg's idea to cause a Drop or Modified Drop sleeve to angle down from the body in a more anatomical manner, and reduce the collection of fabric in the pit.

Two examples of knitting up in color pattern around an armhole to continue the motif unbroken to the cuff: Dive between two stitches and hook up the wools - in pattern - from below. See results on p46. Left: Note the pink crocheted steek. The white running-thread is what hooking-up looks like on the inside.

Knit up stitches around the armhole and mark the exact top stitch which lines up with the shoulder. Establish a CDD *(p24)* at shoulder top as follows: One stitch before the marked stitch, slip 2tog knitwise, k1, p2sso. The resulting single stitch remains the marked stitch. Keep the decreases equidistant, as it might be every 6th or 7th round, depending upon sleeve length, row gauge and the number of stitches to be decreased.

As with single decreases, you must study the situation to see which color will end up being dominant. When working a CDD down the top of a sleeve, the middle stitch (kept always in the same color, let's say dark) will be the winner. If the two colors are strongly contrasting, and if on the preceeding round, the center stitch is flanked by light stitches, knit them in dark, regardless of the pattern, for a smooth CDD with no light peeking through. A side benefit of shaping on the top of the sleeve is the beautiful and surprising looking-glass patterns shown below.

Sleeves from the Cuff

Use EPS on page 43 as a guide for the number of stitches to cast on for the cuff, approx 20-25% of [K]. Work the cuff of your choice. Decide if you want a tapered or a bloused sleeve.

Tapered: Above the cuff, center the motif at sleeve top and count back to find your starting stitch *(see Centering Motifs for Yoke Sweaters p60)*. Mark the 3 underarm sts. Keep them in dark, light, dark (or light, dark, light) throughout the entire sleeve. Increase *(p21)* on each side of the marked stitches every 5th or 6th round to wanted circumference of upper sleeve. Continue straight to wanted length.

Centered Dbl Dec (CDD) down tops of sleeves. Note how patterns blend into ribbing on the 2 righthand models.

Bloused: Above the cuff, increase severely in the first round – as it might be (k2, m1) around. Mark the center 3 underarm sts as above and keep them in alternating vertical stripes. Center the motif at sleeve top *(p60)*, count backward to find your starting stitch and begin motif. Just past elbow length, try the sleeve on and determine how many more stitches you want at upper arm. Establish an increase each side of the 3 marked underarm sts and work them every 5th or 6th round to wanted circumference, then work straight to wanted length.

Join sleeves to body: Rather than sew, you may knit the sleeves into the body as follows. Knit up stitches around the cut armhole to equal the number of stitches at sleeve top. Line up the 2 needles parallel to each other and, beginning at the underarm, work 3-Needle Bind Off *(p39)* from the right side. You can unite the shoulders in the same manner.

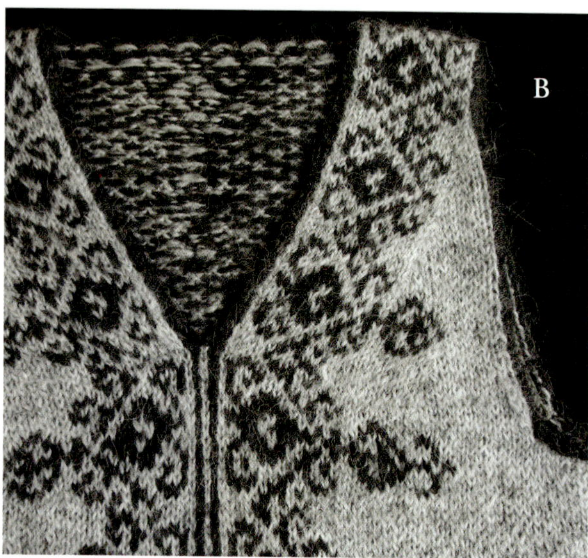

B. EZ's Applied I-Cord borders around V-neck and armholes (Armenian Knitting design)

Armhole Borders for Vests

See, *Ratio of Picked-Up Stitches to Rows* on page 32.

The objective is to have a border that lies nice and flat in relationship to the body - holding in a bit is better than flaring. For fairly wide Vest armhole borders, you may double-decrease at the shoulder tops every other round or so to eliminate "wings".

I-Cord Border for Armhole: Because the armhole (and neck) circumferences are relatively small, an Applied I-Cord border *(p35)* will usually be sufficient to prevent the edges from curling. Either knit up stitches around the opening onto which you will apply I-cord, or apply it directly to the picked up stitch.

Ribbed Border: If your border is corrugated rib, or has a pattern, carefully balance the rib/pattern each side of the proposed dbl-dec points at armhole corners. For example, k2, p2, k1, knit corner marked stitch, k1, p2, k2, etc. Next round, the dbl dec will be worked over the *k1, knit corner marked stitch, k1.* Once established on the first round, the mirror-image will be automatic for the rest of the border *(photo C below).*

Neck Borders

V-Neck Border: Pick up the raw stitches across the neck back. Knit across them, decreasing about 1" worth of stitches on this first pass, to prevent flaring. Now, into the knit-up stitch (cleverly provided in the steek for this purpose), knit up 2 stitches for every 3 rounds (or 3 for 4) down the straight part (if you have one between the V-shaping and the shoulder), then knit up 1 stitch for *every* round along the diagonal V bit. Slide the 3 safety-pin stitches onto the left needle and work a CDD *(p24)* right away. Mirror the knit-up ratio along the other side. Work around in the border of your choice and, on the first round, center the border-pattern each side of the CDD at the apex. We usually work the double-decrease every round.

Crew Neck Border: Knit up all stitches around neck. Decrease across neck-back a bit to prevent flaring. Work border of your choice.

If you choose EZ's Applied I-Cord border *(right)*, it is usually sufficient to prevent the Stocking stitch body from curling. However, you might add **Meg's Speed Bump** between the I-Cord and the body as follows: Knit up stitches *(drawing p32)* between Cord and body all around neck opening, then cast off all those knit up stitches.

Square Neck Border: Knit up all stitches around neck. Establish a CDD *(p24)* at all four corners – or on front corners only for a square front and rounded back.

EZ's Applied I-Cord Border: Pick up about 20 stitches along border *(see rate of pick up on p32)*. On 2nd needle, cast on 2 (or 3) I-Cord stitches and transfer them to the pick-up needle. *K1 (or 2), slip 1, k1 picked up stitch, psso. Replace stitches to left needle and repeat from *. When you have used the 20 stitches you picked up, pick up 20 more, etc. This technique is identical to I-Cord bind off *(p39)*, but you are dealing with a selvedge instead of raw stitches. At the top corner, work an unattached I-Cord before and after the corner stitch, to provide more fabric to swing around the 90-degrees. Now apply a second layer to the first (pick-up rate is 1:1), incorporating EZ's Hidden or Looped I-Cord buttonholes *(p38)*.

Cardigan Borders

Decide on your knit-up mode and ratio *(p32)*. With a 40" or longer circular needle, knit up stitches along one side, around the neck and down the other side. All front opening stitches are on one needle.

Two-Color Pattern border: If knitting a two-color border in the round, knit up all border stitches and work a Wrapped steek *(p18)* at the lower center front.

When buttonholes are done and wanted width is achieved, purl one round and work a solid color facing with matching buttonholes and tack down facing. Cut through Wrapped Steek and darn ends into the tube.

Border Around the Entire Periphery: You may use raw stitches from a Provisional cast on, or pick up from the cast-on selvedge around the lower edge.

Begin at a side seam and knit up 1 for 1 along the lower edge, to the front opening. Continue up one front with whatever ratio you have determined *(p32)*; along the lower neck opening at 1 for 1; up the side of the neck at the same ratio as the front edge; around the neck back at 1 for 1 (to be reduced during a subsequent row) - then mirror-image for the other side of the neck, the other front, and around the rest of the lower edge; miter the corners *(p34, photo A)*.

V-Neck Cardigan Border *(photo 1, p26)*: If the V-neck is narrow, you need not make a corner allowance at the point where the V begins. If you want a sharper angle, mark the corner stitch and increase 1 st each side of it every 4th row. Decrease slightly across the neck-back on your first row, to prevent flaring.

Crew Neck *(photo A, p34)*: Mark the two top corners and work an increase each side of the marked stitch every-other-row. Skip the final increase for gently rounded corners. If you purl the marked stitch on the way back, you will get a nice Stocking stitch detail. Decrease gently across the neck-back on the first pass. Add buttonholes near the half-way point. I-Cord Bind Off is very good looking on a Garter stitch border *(p39)*.

Square Neck: As well as increasing at the center front corners, make a CDD *(p24)* dart at the inside corners, as follows: knit to within 1 stitch of marked inner corner, slip 2tog knitwise, k1, p2sso. If you purl those marked stitches on the inside, you get nice diagonal lines of Stocking stitch on the outside.

Hidden I-Cord buttonholes between 2 layers of Applied I-Cord

Buttonholes

Generally speaking, buttonholes are worked near the middle of the cardigan border. If the holes are too close to the outer edge, the band may become scalloped with wear.

Spacing Buttonholes: Mary Rowe, author of *Knitted Tams*, came up with an excellent formula for plotting evenly-spaced buttonholes:

$$S = \frac{N - (H \times B) - E}{B - 1}$$

S = number of stitches between buttonholes
N = total number of stitches
H = number of stitches in each buttonhole
B = number of wanted buttonholes
E = stitches remaining at ends of button band

Try it, it works beautifully.

Medrith Glover's Buttonhole for Corrugated Rib: Depending on your gauge, the following 6-stitch buttonhole measures about 3/4". Each buttonhole is worked on a right side row without turning the work. Each buttonhole happens in a 6-stitch (p2, k2, p2) space, so mark the appropriate stitches, right side for women, left side for men.

On right side, work in pattern to first buttonhole location.

1. Using purl color, bind off 6 stitches in purl.
2. Place remaining stitch back on left needle.
3. Cable cast-on 7 stitches.
4. Undo last ribbed stitch on right needle and place old stitch onto left needle.
5. With knit color, work ssk with old stitch and extra cast-on stitch.
6. Re-establish Corrugated rib in both colors on the 6 new buttonhole stitches.
7. Slip next stitch to right needle and with left needle, from behind, snag lefthand side of stitch below the one you just slipped, replace slipped stitch to left needle and k2tog. Work rib to next buttonhole.

Medrith's buttonhole

EZ's One-Row-Buttonhole, 3 Stitches Wide: On right side, work in pattern to first buttonhole location.

1. Slip 1 purlwise.
2. Take wool to front, between needles, and drop it.
3. Slip 1 purlwise, pass slipped stitch over.
4. Slip 1 purlwise, pass slipped stitch over.
5. Slip 1 purlwise, pass slipped stitch over.
6. Twist stitch on L needle.
7. Twist stitch on R needle.
8. Pull working wool tightly and lay over R needle.
9. Pass slipped stitch over it.
10. Make 4 firm backward loops over R needle.
11. K2tog.

When working the above in two colors, carry both working strands together as one throughout the instructions *(thank you, Kevin Ames)*.

I-Cord Buttonhole, EZ's Hidden: Work EZ's Applied I-Cord *(p35)* along a selvedge. When you get to where you'd like a Hidden Buttonhole, work 3 rounds of I-Cord (more or less, depending upon wanted size) without attaching. Slide 3 of the picked-up stitches off the left needle and continue Applied I-Cord to the next buttonhole site.

I-Cord Buttonhole, EZ's Looped: As above -- when you get to the right spot, work 6 to 8 rounds of I-Cord without attaching (depending upon wanted button-hole size). Resume Applied I-Cord and you will have a nice loop (drawing below).

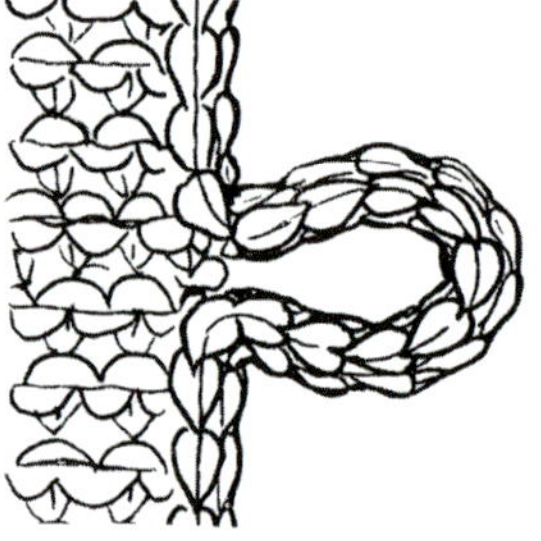

To prevent this buttonhole from stretching, wrap the working wool around it's base two or three times before continuing, as in photo below, right.

Instant Small Buttonhole: Yarn Over, k2tog.

shoulder shaping on Ann Feitelson's "Shirt Tail" design

I-Cord Loop buttonhole (and After-Thought Pocket)

Bind Off or Cast Off

I-Cord Bind-Off: This puts a tiny tube of Stocking stitch along a selvedge. On the left needle are raw stitches; onto the right needle, cast on 2 (or 3) stitches. Transfer them to the left needle and *knit 1 (or 2), k2tog through-back-loops (being the last Cord stitch and one of the raw or knitted-up stitches). Replace the 2 (or 3) stitches to left needle and repeat from *.

You can clip along at great speed by not replacing the last Cord stitch to the left needle; leave it on the right needle, insert the tip of the left needle into it and knit the next round. Yes, that will twist the first stitch of every round but when worked consistently, it looks very nice.

Uniting Two Sections of Knitting

3-Needle Bind-Off: This method may be worked from the outside or inside of the garment. You can use it to unite shoulders as follows: put all front stitches on one needle and all back stitches on a second needle. With the third needle, k2tog (one stitch each from front and back needles). *K2tog, pass last stitch over. Repeat from * across all raw stitches. If worked from the outside, this technique produces a ridge. If worked from the inside, the outside resembles a woven seam. You will notice that the front and back have different appearances, so, for uniformity work each shoulder in the same direction: from armhole to neck edge, then from neck edge to armhole. (Or work the opposite shoulder in the same direction as the first, but p2tog instead of knit.)

You may also use this technique to knit a sleeve into an armhole as follows: have the raw sleeve stitches on one needle, knit up stitches around armhole opening on another needle and unite them with the third needle. When done from the outside of the garment, this produces a handsome ridge, which will match the above shoulder join - and may be worked in a continuous line.

3-Needle I-Cord Bind-Off: As above, but establish a 2-stitch I-Cord before you begin. Then *k1 Cord stitch, slip 1, k2tog (from front and back needle), psso, replace Cord stitches to one of the left needles and repeat from *.

Grafting, Weaving, Kitchener Stitch

Yes, a confusing assortment of names for an invaluable technique. The most common uses are to weave the underarm of a yoke sweater (which makes the garment totally seamless), shoulders of a vest, top of a hood and the toes of socks.

We do not recommend weaving shoulders except on a vest, or if you are using a fine, lightweight wool. A heavier sleeve will drag and stretch a woven shoulder seam, so use non-stretch 3-Needle bind-off *(p39)*, or simply sew the seam.

Weaving effectively knits two pieces of fabric together; use a blunt sewing-up needle. This operation may be worked on or off the needles and each stitch - except the first and last - is dealt with twice.

Weaving Off the Needles: Arrange the two pieces as in the drawing *(right)* and, beginning on the right-hand end: Come up through the first stitch on the lower piece and up through the first stitch on the upper piece. That aligns the ends. Now ...

Lower Stitches: *Go down into the first stitch and come up into the second from below. Pull the wool through - leaving it loose.

Upper Stitches: Repeat from * above.

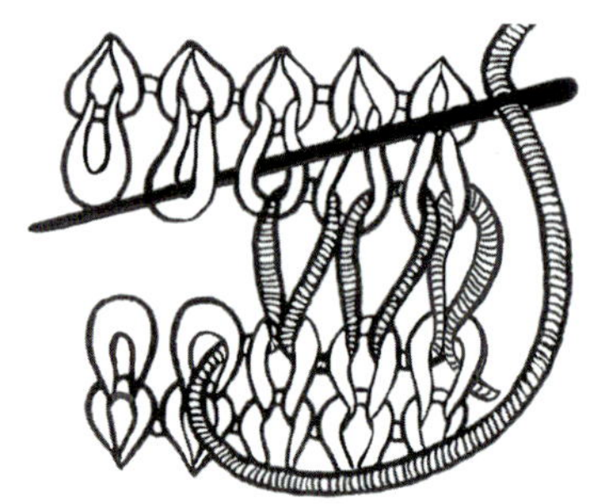

Weaving Stocking stitch, off the needles.

Now continue across: Go down into the stitch you came out of last time and up into the next stitch.

Weaving On the Needles: Although you are achieving the identical result, the song is different. Hold needles parallel with insides of work together. Line up the ends as follows: go through the first stitch on the lower needle as if to purl; go through the first stitch on the upper needle as if to knit. Pull the wool through. Now ...

Lower Needle: **Go through the first stitch as if to knit, slide it off the needle. Go through the second stitch as if to purl, leave it on. Pull the wool through.
Upper Needle: Go through the first stitch as if to purl, slide it off. Go through the second stitch as if to knit, leave it on. Pull the wool through.
Repeat from **. Isn't it wonderful?

vest seam woven at shoulder top, in the plain row between OXOs

vest seam placed behind the shoulder top and woven on a plain row between motifs

Weaving on the needles, abbreviated,
Lower: As if to knit, off - as if to purl, pull through.
Upper: As if to purl, off - as if to knit, pull through.

As you become more proficient and relaxed, you will compose your own song to accompany the moves; a kind of weaving mantra.

Tip: During the actual weaving, you have enough to do without worrying about matching gauge, so keep the weaving loose and snug it up - stitch by stitch - after you are through. It is easier to begin neatening at the center of the weaving and even up the stitches toward each edge.

Sometimes you need to unite live stitches to a selvedge. You can do a kind of half-weave by following the above instructions on the raw stitches and simply looping in and out through the selvedge. Experiment and see what looks best.

To Weave With Two Colors: It is much easier to weave a solid color. In the photos on page 40, the two fronts are woven to the backs in the plain round between patterns.

Sometimes the motifs are entwined and you must weave across a patterned row. In that case, weave all stitches with the predominant color, then work duplicate stitch to insert the second shade.

Weaving Underarms of Yoke Sweater: Each end of the weave requires extra attention to eliminate the inevitable hole that appears. See the third paragraph on page 45.

Finishing Up

Washing Tips: Use pure soap and medium temperature water. Submerge the knitted item into the soapy water and let it sit for 5 minutes. Squeeze (do not wring) out water; rinse; squeeze and rinse again. Spin in wash machine for a minute or two. Remove and block.

Blocking Tips: Never use pins if you can avoid them (except for lace borders). Take the clean, damp sweater and flop it onto a towel on the kitchen table. Arrange and pat it into shape.

Since a damp 100% wool sweater is rather like putty, you can bend it to your will. Measure sleeves and body and make any necessary adjustments as follows: yank on bottom of sleeves or body to make them longer (and narrower). Pull the body or sleeves sideways to make them wider (and shorter).

When nearly dry, flip it over onto a fresh towel to dry the other side.

Steam Block: Smooth the knitting with a steam iron held just above the surface of the fabric.

Chapter 3: Design Your Own

Designing an allover color patterned garment is actually quite straight forward. Armed with your proper gauge and the dimensions you want to knit, you can make some decisions, do a tiny bit of math, then cast on and knit.

Step 1 - Know Your Gauge

At the beginning of this book we gave details on working various gauge-checking projects. When designing your own garment, you needn't match the gauge of a written pattern. Therefore, a gauge with odd numbers (such as 23 sts/4 inches) is fine. You don't need to work hard to get to 24/4, because you are in charge.

Step 2 - Know Your Goal Measurements

Pick a favorite-fitting sweater and note the circumference, the length to underarm, sleeve length, upper arm circumference, and neck width.

Resist the temptation to use a sweatshirt as your guide. Heavy commercial fabric has a completely different drape from two-color handknitted fabric.

One of the things that makes us love our favorite-fitting sweater is the amount of ease that was built into it. Ease is the difference between your actual measurement and the garment's measurement.

Design Choices

Cast On	Lower Edge	Armhole Shape	Neck Shape	Sleeves
German Twisted	Corrugated Rib	Drop Shoulder	Crew Neck	No Sleeves
Austrian	Checkerboard	Modified Drop	Square Neck	Top Down
Cable	Purl-when-you-can	Gusset	V-Neck	Cuff Up
Other	Hem	Half-Gusset	Other	
	Other	Shaped (Vest)		
		Square (Vest)		
		Set-In Sleeve		
		Other		

cutting a crocheted steek

As a guideline, use the following numbers to figure an ease amount.

Form Fitting: Make the sweater 1 to 2 inches *smaller* than your measurements.

Slim/Average Fit: Add about 2 inches to your body measurements.

Loose/Relaxed Fit: Add 3 to 4 inches to your actual body measurements.

Oversized Fit: Add 5 to 6 inches to your actual body measurements.

Step 3 - Make Some Choices

You need to make a few basic choices at the outset. First, decide if your garment will have a center-front opening or not. You need to accommodate steek stitches if you're making a cardigan. Then, select one item from each of the columns in the Design Choices box on the previous page.

Step 4 - Plan Your Cast On Number

Use the chart below with your wanted circumference and gauge. If you are making a cardigan, add steek stitches to the number you are casting on.

The chart indicates how many to cast on (assuming you want 10% fewer stitches around the lower border), followed by the number to increase to for the body. Round up or down to suit the stitch pattern you choose; for example, in case you need the number to be divisibly by 4 or 6.

To evenly space the increase into the cast on number, see the More-or-Less right formula on page 19.

Step 5 - Use EPS (Elizabeth's Percentage System) to Plan the Garment

EPS was devised by Elizabeth Zimmermann to produce a custom-fitted garment based upon knowledge of your gauge and the wanted chest circumference.

Multiply your gauge times the wanted number of inches around the chest. That number is referred to as the Key Number or [K], which is 100%. If any of the numbers in the chart below fit your wanted gauge and size, use them. When using EPS with this chart, the number you "Inc to" is your key number [K].

Chart on numbers for circumference and gauge combinations.

Size	6 stitches to 1"	6.5 stitches to 1"	7 stitches to 1"	7.5 stitches to 1"	8 stitches to 1"
36"	CO 192 Inc to 216	CO 212 Inc to 234	CO 228 Inc to 252	CO 244 Inc to 270	CO 260 Inc to 288
40"	CO 216 Inc to 240	CO 232 Inc to 260	CO 252 Inc to 280	CO 272 Inc to 300	CO 288 Inc to 320
44"	CO 236 Inc to 264	CO 256 Inc to 286	CO 280 Inc to 308	CO 296 Inc to 330	CO 316 Inc to 352
48"	CO 256 Inc to 288	CO 280 Inc to 312	CO 304 Inc to 336	CO 324 Inc to 360	CO 348 Inc to 384
52"	CO 280 Inc to 312	CO 304 Inc to 338	CO 328 Inc to 364	CO 352 Inc to 390	CO 374 Inc to 416
56"	CO 304 Inc to 336	CO 328 Inc to 364	CO 352 Inc to 392	CO 378 Inc to 420	CO 404 Inc to 448
60"	CO 324 Inc to 360	CO 352 Inc to 390	CO 378 Inc to 420	CO 404 Inc to 450	CO 432 Inc to 480

EPS Yoke Pullover: A seamless garment with no steeks or cutting, so perhaps a good place to begin.

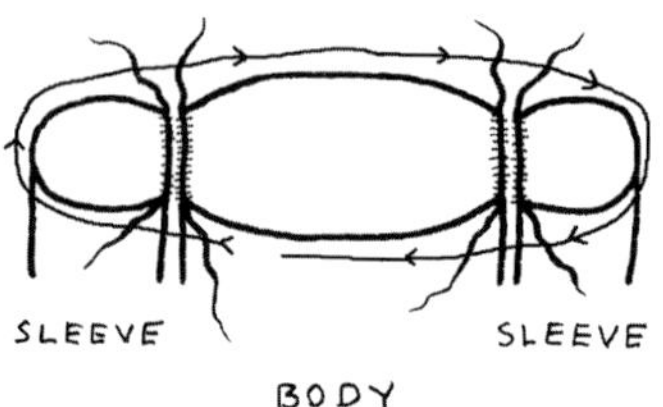

Work a lower border treatment, then increase to body circumference. Shape body to underarms *(see Body Shaping, p51)*, if wanted and put underarm stitches on a thread.

Begin sleeves at the cuff and choose the shape you want; tapered or bloused *(pp33-34)*. Inc to wanted upper arm circumference and put underarm stitches on a thread.

Match up the underarm stitches-on-a-thread and unite sleeves to body as in the drawing. Now all stitches – minus 4 groups of underarm stitches – are on one needle.

Work at least 2 plain rounds to get everybody settled down and insert 3 to 4 sets of short rows *(p29)* to raise the neck back - and lower the neck front.

Follow left side of yoke schematic below, with 3 rings of decreases, if upper arm is about 33-35% of [K]. If the upper arm is around 40% of [K], follow right side of schematic with 4 rings of decreases as you have more stitches to eliminate.

The decreases may be placed between rings of color pattern motifs, or the decreases may be incorporated into the motifs as part of the pattern.

EPS *(Elizabeth's Percentage System)* for a Seamless Yoke

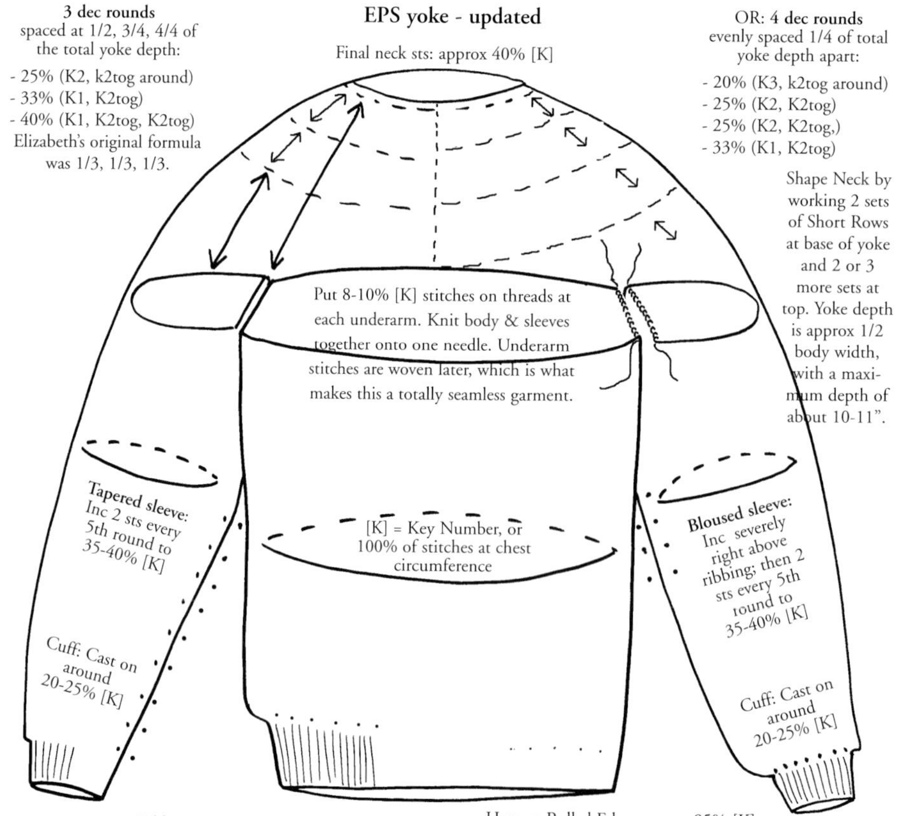

3 dec rounds
spaced at 1/2, 3/4, 4/4 of the total yoke depth:
- 25% (K2, k2tog around)
- 33% (K1, K2tog)
- 40% (K1, K2tog, K2tog)

Elizabeth's original formula was 1/3, 1/3, 1/3.

EPS yoke - updated

Final neck sts: approx 40% [K]

OR: **4 dec rounds**
evenly spaced 1/4 of total yoke depth apart:
- 20% (K3, k2tog around)
- 25% (K2, K2tog)
- 25% (K2, K2tog,)
- 33% (K1, K2tog)

Shape Neck by working 2 sets of Short Rows at base of yoke and 2 or 3 more sets at top. Yoke depth is approx 1/2 body width, with a maximum depth of about 10-11".

Put 8-10% [K] stitches on threads at each underarm. Knit body & sleeves together onto one needle. Underarm stitches are woven later, which is what makes this a totally seamless garment.

Tapered sleeve: Inc 2 sts every 5th round to 35-40% [K]

Bloused sleeve: Inc severely right above ribbing; then 2 sts every 5th round to 35-40% [K]

[K] = Key Number, or 100% of stitches at chest circumference

Cuff: Cast on around 20-25% [K]

Cuff: Cast on around 20-25% [K]

Ribbing or garter-stitch, cast on 90% [K]. Inc to 100% in first round above lower edge.

Hem or Rolled Edge, cast on 95% [K]. Increase to 100% above rolled edge - or in pairs at side "seams" as you work up the body.

For a wider neck opening, eliminate the final dec, or reduce the number of stitches decreased.

Around the neck, work ribbing, or a hem, or a Garter stitch border *(pp34-35)*.

The part that makes this a seamless garment is weaving *(p40)* the underarms. Line up body and sleeve stitches-on-a-thread onto a pair of dp needles. To prevent holes at each corner, pick up a loose strand at each end of each needle, twist it and put it onto the needle as a stitch. So if you had 13 sts on each needle, now you have 15.

To center any pattern on a yoke, see page 60.

Instead of concentric rings (as on the pink-yoke sweater below), the decreases between underarm and neck are worked in vertical lines. More yoke photos on pp36-37.

EPS *Modified* Dropped-Shoulder Pullover: Work the body from lower edge to underarm. Determine the number of inches you want the sleeves inset into the body, possibly as far as the recipient's shoulder point. Put double that number of stitches on a thread for each armhole; half for front and half for back. Cast on steek stitches and continue around to base of neck. You may shape the armhole by putting fewer stitches on a thread, and decreasing the armhole each side of the steek for the first few inches *(p25)*. Work the neck steek and continue to shoulder height.

Secure and cut armhole and neck openings. Unite shoulder seam. Knit up stitches around armhole and work sleeve to cuff, shaping down sleeve top, or along underarm. Or knit sleeve up from the cuff, and knit it into the armhole with 3-Needle bind off *(p39)*.

EPS Straight Drop-Shoulder Pullover: Work as for EPS Modified-Drop *(p45)*, except make no allowance for the sleeve as you work your way from lower edge to bottom of neck opening; work neck steek.

Sleeves are knitted up from the cuff and cast off. Measure sleeve top against the side of the body and mark the sleeve depth. Secure the armhole stitches and cut open. Unite the shoulder seam to form an armhole.

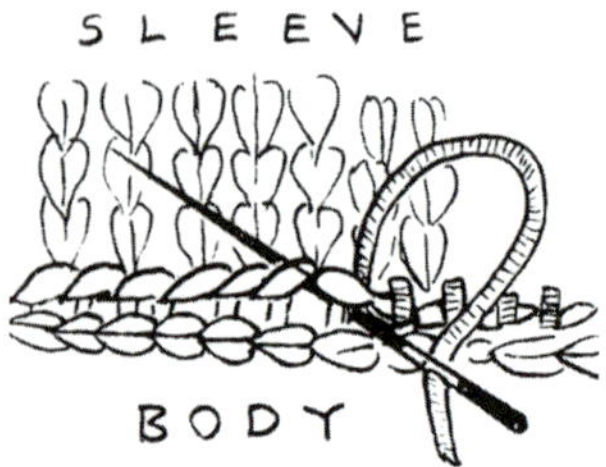

Pin the sleeve top to the shoulder seam, the underarm to the pit. Now pin at the halfway points and the quarters as well, if you like. Assign a sewing-up stitch each side of armhole and, from the right side, sew the sleeve into the body *(above)*. Since the armhole stretched slightly upon being cut open, you will ease the body onto the sleeve; watch carefully and take a bigger bite of body when necessary to match the pinned segments.

Four examples of sweaters with square, diagonal yoke motifs. Turn the chart on its ear and knit up around the cut armhole in color-pattern (p32). The armhole seam is nearly indetectable. Work sleeve to cuff, CDD down the top of the sleeve (photo p33).

EPS *(Elizabeth's Percentage System)* for Drop or Modified Drop-Shoulder

Boat Neck: At shoulder height, sew up 1/4 body width for each shoulder. Work Hem or knit Norwegian stand-up neck.

Scoop Neck: 2-3" shy of wanted length, put center sts on thread. Cast on 5-7 steek sts. Continue (shaping or not) to shoulder.

machine-stitching

Pin sleeve into armhole and sew in. Or *knit it* in. You may pick up sts around armhole and knit sleeve down but pattern stitches will be on their heads.

Norwegian Drop-Shoulder: Work straight from lower edge to shoulder.

Modified Drop-Shoulder: Decide wanted depth of inset, and put corresponding sts on thread at u-arm. Cast on 5-7 steek sts, and continue to neck opening.

Work top of sleeve back and forth to match depth of inset armhole. OR, knit up all armhole sts and work a half-gusset, then decrease to cuff.

100% = [K]

Bloused Sleeve: Cast on 20-25% [K]. Inc severely above ribbing. Work straight to around elbow height. Inc 1 st each side of center 3 u-arm sts to wanted circumference (45-50% [K]). Work straight to wanted length.

Tapered Sleeve: Cast on 20-25% [K]. Mark center 3 u-arm sts. Inc 1 stitch each side of marked sts every 4th or 5th rnd to wanted circ: 45-50% [K]. Work straight to wanted length.

Ribbed border: Cast on 90% of [K]. Inc.10% above rib.

Hemmed border: Cast on 95% of [K]. Inc at sides. Knit actual hem after garment is finished.

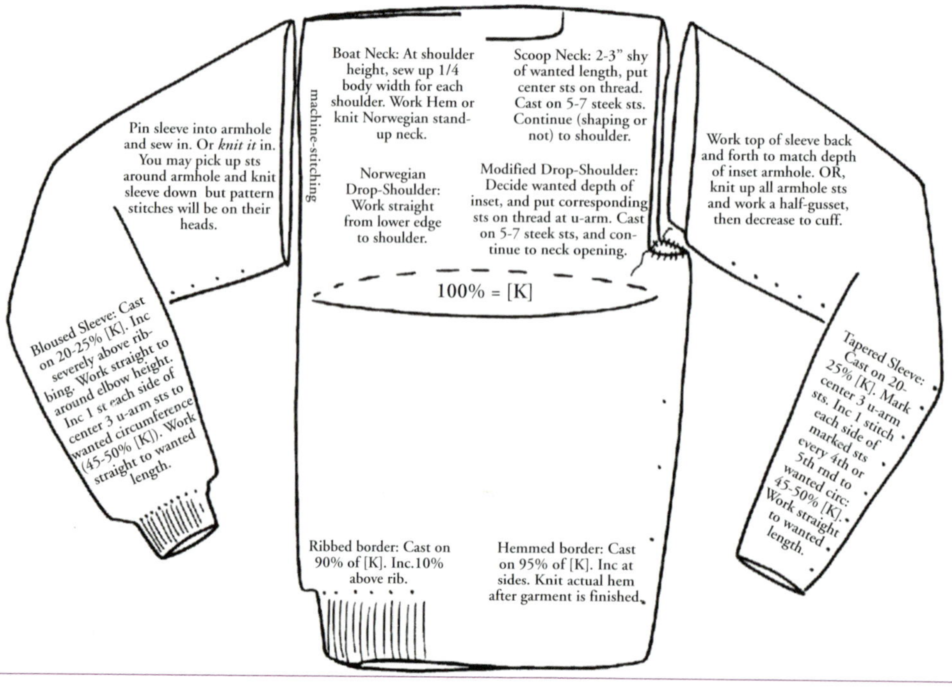

Using Pivot Stitches

When the number of stitches you have around the body is not divisible by the pattern-repeat, or if you want to shape the body, or if you want to assure that the motifs will meet perfectly at the shoulder top, a Pivot Stitch at each side "seam" is necessary. They will divide front from back resulting in a mirror-imaged motif.

Pivot Stitch Choices (see below):

- (A) a single, neutral stitch separating front from back; kept in background color throughout.
- (B) 3 sts at each side seam; kept in vertical stripes, or a different motif entirely (see next page), with the main body patterns balanced on each side. Use more than 3 sts if you like.
- (C) a single stitch in pattern, which is the last stitch on the front AND the first stitch on the back; a shared stitch.

Pullover: When setting up an all-over design, the crucial thing is to have the motif centered on front and back *(p49)*. Once that is established, it does not matter where the motif stops at the side seams, as long as it is identical each side of the Pivot Stitch.

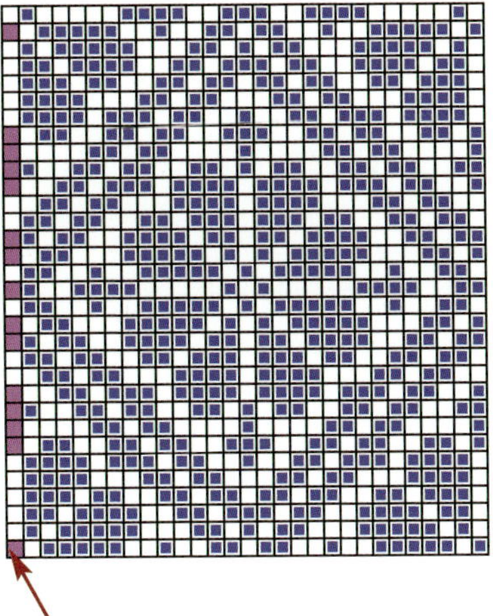

*Pivot Stitch on one repeat of the motif (shown in a different color for clarity). It is actually the last stitch of this repeat **and** the first stitch of the next repeat.*

If the L and R halves of each front and back motif mirror each other, you only need to follow a relatively narrow chart of 1/4 of the circumference. Beginning at a side seam: *Read the chart line from R to L and you are at center front (or back). Read the same line from L to R and you are at the other side seam. Repeat from * and you are back at the beginning of the round. Move your Magnetic Row Finder up and repeat for the next line on the chart.

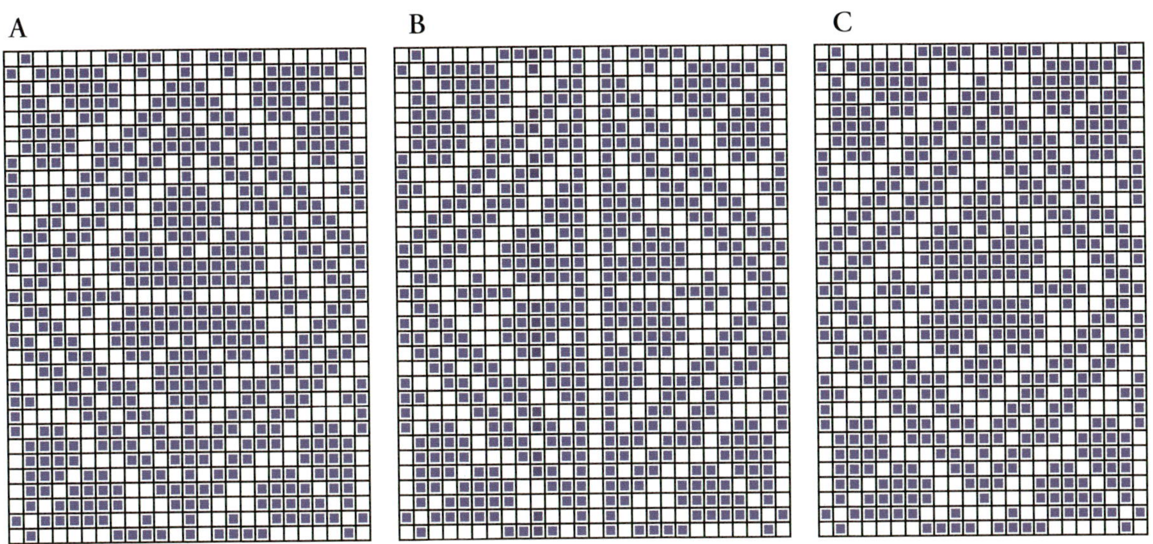

Three types of Pivot Stitches: (A) One solid pattern-color stitch throughout. (B) Three stitches kept in dark, light, dark throughout. (C) A single pattern stitch shared by both L and R sides.

D

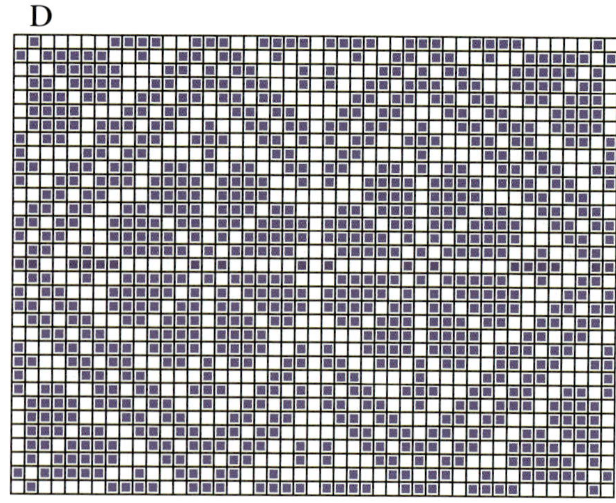

Cardigan: When setting up an all-over design, the motif must be centered at the back. To have the front and back align at the shoulders, the side "seams" must be mirror-imaged, as in examples A - F.

Partial motifs are wonderful and, when separated only by a Pivot Stitch, form a lovely Rorschach pattern of their own.

See the photos below for side panels and a Pivot Stitch in action at side seams.

E panel sts

F panel sts

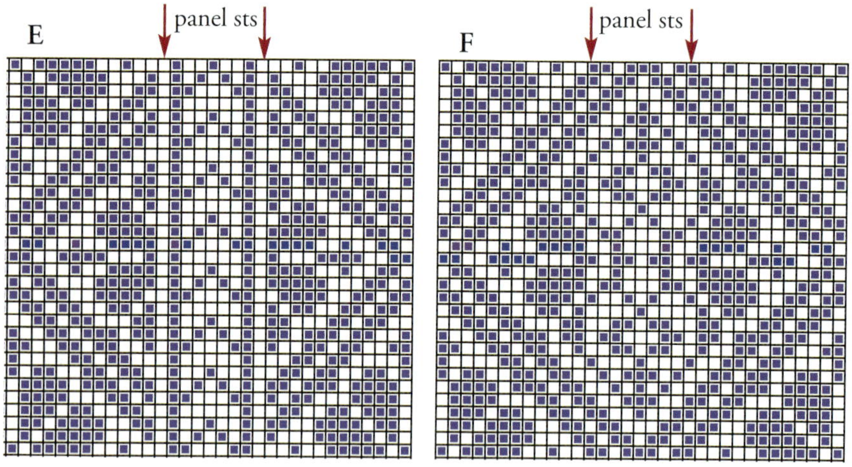

D *shows a single background color seam stitch.*

E *has a separate motif panel at the side.*

F *the "panel" sts in E are turned into a pattern that merges with the motif.*

The examples on these two pages are possibilities for you to experiment with.

Side seams L to R: 7-stitch striped seam, single pivot stitch, 5-stitch striped seam, 17-stitch panel pattern with signature.

Centering Any Color Pattern

When you design your own color-patterned sweater and try to fit a large repeat motif into a specific number of stitches, there is a high probability that the pattern will not fit evenly into the stitch count. To center a yoke or sleeves, see page 60.

If you are fairly close to your wanted numbers, you can alter your gauge and/or stitch count slightly to make it come out evenly.

Patterns in books always have the motif and stitch count worked out for you. However, you are now designing your own sweater and the following steps (developed by Cully Swansen), will allow you to fit any color pattern into any stitch count and center the patterns perfectly.

Two variables come into play: Does your pattern repeat have a single center stitch, or 2 center sts (see Charts 1 and 2, below)? Are you knitting a steeked cardigan or a pullover?

For either a pullover or a cardigan, begin with A, B and C:

A. Multiply wanted circumference times established gauge.

B. Subtract the side seam stitches. ***Seam could be a single pivot stitch, 3 stitch stripes, or a wide panel; see pages 47-48 .***

C. Adjust the resulting number (round up or down) to be divisible by 4.

For a motif with a *single* center stitch (Chart 1)

Pullover: After A, B, C,

D. Add 2 sts to provide a center stitch on both front and back.

E. Add the side seam stitches back in (the ones you removed in step B); this is the number to cast on.

F. To find the starting stitch on your pattern repeat, first divide the number from step **C** by 4.

G. Then divide the resulting number by the number of sts in the pattern-repeat and note the left-over stitches, if any.

H. Finally, count the left-over number from L to R on the pattern repeat; that is your starting stitch. If no stitches were left over, start at the lower right corner of the pattern repeat, see Note in box below.

Start the round at a side seam. Work seam, then begin at your starting stitch and follow chart from R to L to center back.

After knitting the center-back stitch (which is the lower right corner stitch of your chart; the *center-front and -back stitch* on Chart 3, page 50), read the same chart line from L to R to the other seam; do not repeat center-back stitch. Work seam and read same line from R to L to center front. Read same line from L to R to beginning of round. Move row-finder up one line on chart and continue.

Cardigan: After A, B, C,

D. Subtract 1 stitch to create a center-back stitch.

E. Add the side seam stitches back in (the ones you

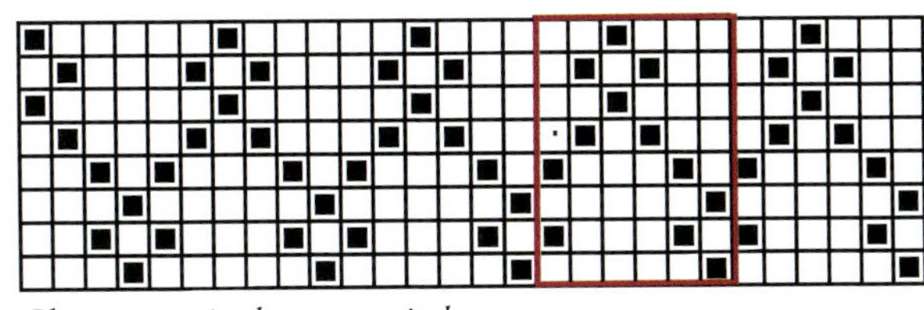

Chart 1, *a single center stitch.*

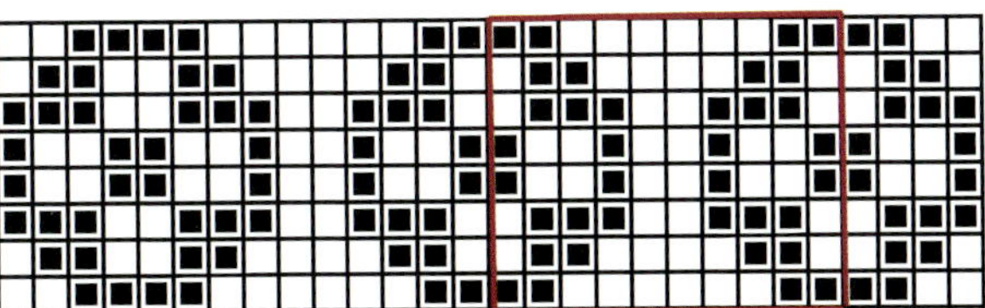

Chart 2, *double center stitches.*

Note: When marking the pattern repeat on the chart, make the single "center" stitch the righthand edge, as in Chart 1.

For double center sts, one of the "center" sts is on the right side; the other on the left side of the repeat, as in Chart 2.

If you'd like to knit a quick cap to practice Cully's Pattern Centering concept, see page 56.

To center a yoke or sleeves, see page 60.

removed in step B); this is the number to cast on, plus the number wanted for the steek.

Start round at right front (just past center steek) with *beginning and center-back stitch* (see Chart 4 below). Read the chart from R to L to side seam. Seam could be a single pivot stitch, 3 stitch stripes or a wide panel.

After working seam, begin with the same stitch you ended on before seam and read the chart from L to R to the center back.

After knitting the center-back stitch, read the same chart line from R to L to the other side seam (do not repeat center-back stitch).

After seam, read the chart from L to R to the steek. (The last stitch of the round is identical to the first; that is the reason for the "subtract 1" on a cardigan; there is an odd number of stitches on the back and an even number on the front.) Work steek and move up to the next row on the chart.

For a motif with *two* center stitches (Chart 2)

Begin with A, B, C *(p49),*

D. Add the side seam stitches back in (the ones you removed in step B); this is the number to cast on (plus steek stitches if making a cardigan). Mark the 2 center-back stitches.

Pullover:

E. To find the starting stitch on your pattern repeat,

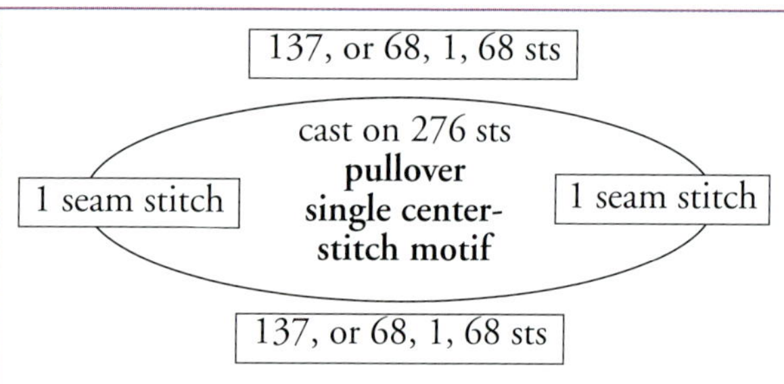

A. 42" **pullover** @ 6.5 sts to 1" = 273 sts.
B. Minus the seam sts (2) = 271 sts.
C. Make it divisible by 4 (272).
D. Add 2 for front and back center sts = 274.
E. Add side seam sts (2) = 276.
F & G. 68 ÷ 26-stitch repeat = 2 full repeats + 16 sts left.

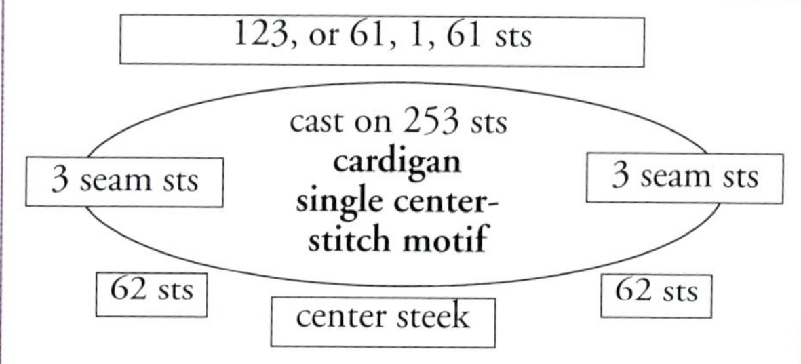

A. 39" **cardigan** @ 6.5 sts to 1" = 253.5 sts.
B. Minus the seam sts (6) = 247.5 sts.
C. Make it divisible by 4 (248).
D. Subtract 1 to create a center-back stitch = 247.
E. Add side seam sts (6) = 253.
Begin round just past the center steek.

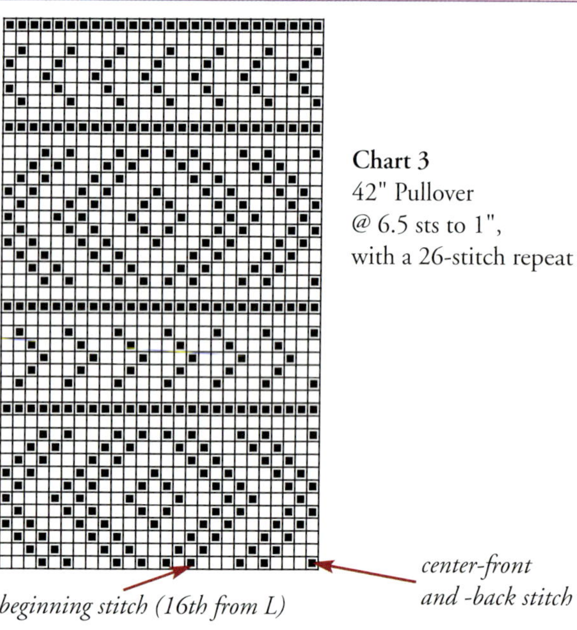

Chart 3
42" Pullover
@ 6.5 sts to 1",
with a 26-stitch repeat

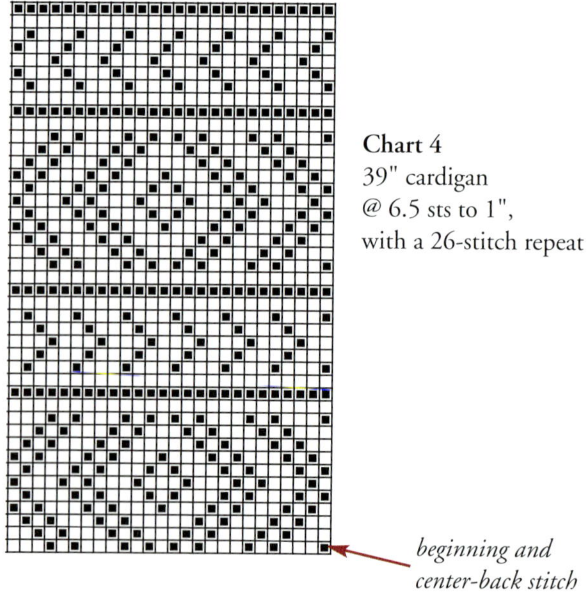

Chart 4
39" cardigan
@ 6.5 sts to 1",
with a 26-stitch repeat

first divide the number from step **C** by 4.

F. Divide the resulting number by the number of sts in the pattern-repeat and note the left-over stitches, if any.

G. Finally, count the left-over number from L to R on the pattern repeat; that is your starting stitch. If no stitches were left over, start at the lower right corner of the pattern repeat. See Note in box on page 49.

Work side seam, then begin at your starting stitch and follow chart from R to L. Stop after knitting first center-back stitch.

Read the same chart line from L to R (repeat the stitch you ended on). Work to the other seam.

Complete the round as established. Move row-finder up one line on chart and continue.

Cardigan: Begin round at the right front (just past center steek) and, starting at lower right corner of the chart, read the chart from R to L to seam. After working seam, begin exactly where you left the chart before seam and read the chart from L to R to the center back. Read the same chart line from R to L (repeat the stitch you ended on) to the other seam. After seam, read the chart from L to R to the steek. Work steek and move up to the next row on the chart.

Body Shaping

A fitted body is very fashionable these days. The chart below is an example of what a chart with a 5-stitch side seam might look like if you decrease to the waist, then increase to the chest. Naturally, your inc and dec rate may be different *(see Row Gauge, pp10-11)*.

Armholes

OK. You've cast on, worked the lower edge and increased to full body circumference . . .

Traditional Drop Shoulders: Knit body right up to the bottom of the proposed neck opening and establish a steek there. When the cuff-up sleeves are finished, measure the depth of the sleeve top against the side of the body and mark where to machine stitch and cut. This is often referred to as a "straight-drop-shoulder" *(see EPS schematic on p46)*.

Alternately, knit to the bottom of the future armhole, put 1 stitch on a coilless pin at underarm and cast on a steek for future cutting *(p25)*. Then work straight to bottom of the neck opening.

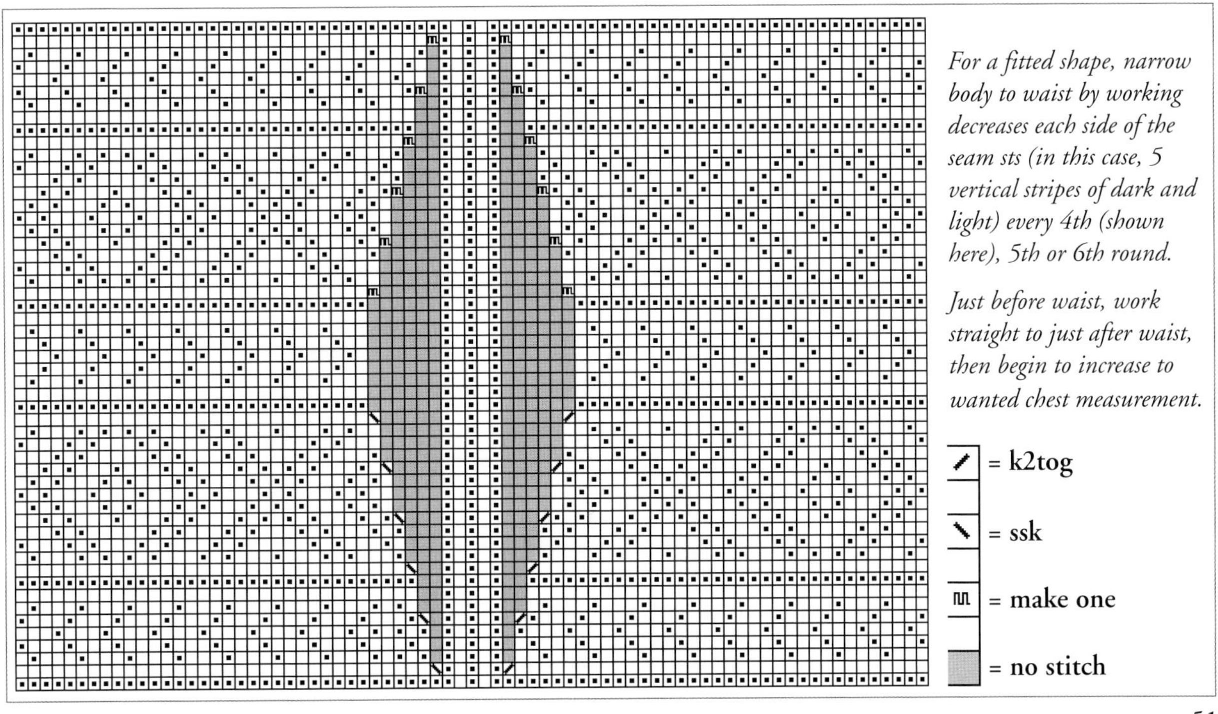

For a fitted shape, narrow body to waist by working decreases each side of the seam sts (in this case, 5 vertical stripes of dark and light) every 4th (shown here), 5th or 6th round.

Just before waist, work straight to just after waist, then begin to increase to wanted chest measurement.

Modified (Inset) Drop Shoulder: Knit body to wanted length to underarm. Decide how far you want the sleeve inset into the body (maybe 2" - depending upon the incidence of pattern) and put double that distance (4" worth) of underarm stitches onto a thread (2" each side of seam stitch) and add steek stitches *(see Kangaroo Pouch, p25)*. Work to bottom of neck opening.

Or, you may nearly duplicate the appearance of a Set-In Sleeve with this method: Calculate shoulder width by measuring the recipient from shoulder point to shoulder point across the front. Subtract that width from body width and divide in half. Follow instructions for the shaped vest armhole, ahead.

Gusset or Half-Gusset: Knit body until 3 or 4" before wanted length to underarm. Begin to increase one stitch each side of each marked side seam stitch every 3rd round.

If you begin 4" from underarm and are getting 7 rounds per inch, you will have approximately 21 gusset stitches: 10 pairs of inc + a center stitch. Inc in rounds 1, 4, 7, 10, 13, etc.

If you begin 3" from underarm and are getting 7 rounds per inch, you will end up with 17 gusset stitches (8 pairs of inc + center st). Either incorporate the increased stitches into the main design, or keep them in stripes, or knit a totally different motif just for the gusset.

At the underarm, put only the increased gusset stitches (and the center one) on a thread and cast on steek stitches. You can either reverse this gusset shape as you work the sleeve to the cuff. Or, don't work a gusset on the body, but place one on the sleeve for a Half-Gusset. Work body to bottom of neck opening.

Shaped Vest Armhole: Knit body to wanted length to underarm. EZ's formula was to get rid of approximately 15% of body stitches at each armhole.

For a curved armhole, put 10% of body stitches onto a thread at each underarm, centered above seam stitches. Cast on steek stitches *(p25)*. Shape each side of the steek (k2tog, k steek, ssk - or reverse the direction of the decreases if that is your preference) until an additional (approximately) 5% of stitches have been consumed; adjust that number to correspond to final wanted shoulder width - taking Vest armhole trim into account. We usually decrease every 2nd round for half the stitches then slow down to every 3rd round for the rest of them; OR, dec every round for half the stitches, then every other round for the rest.

You may want a square armhole, in which case, put approximately 15% of body stitches on a thread at each underarm, add steek stitches and continue to bottom of neck opening without shaping.

Neck Shape

Pullover V-Neck: How deep do you want the V? How wide do you want the top of the V? At what angle do you want the V to slope? What final border will you use and how much will it "fill in" the neck opening? Whatever you decide, when you reach the beginning of the V, put 1, 2 or 3 center-front stitches onto a coilless pin and cast on steek stitches.

Assign a Knit-Up stitch each side of the steek which will be kept in background color throughout and remain uninvolved in the color-pattern *(p15)*.

Angle of V: Decrease each side of the V (k2tog, k steek stitches, ssk) and your rate of decrease will determine the angle: Every 2nd round for a relatively wide V; every 3rd round for a standard V (if there is such a thing as "standard") or every 4th round for a straighter, narrower V. Whichever you choose, continue decreasing until the V is the width you want (here you have to decide what kind of final border may fill in the neck opening). When you have achieved wanted width for top of V, continue the neck straight to wanted height to shoulder.

Cardigan V-Neck: There is no need to form a second steek at the beginning of the V; just shape each side of established center-front steek, see Angle of V above.

Cardigan Crew Neck: How deep and how wide do you want the neck opening? Do you want the corners to be square or curved? What final border will you use and how much will it "fill in" the neck opening?

If you are knitting a cardigan, there will be an additional steek for a Crew neck. Depending upon your gauge, calculate the number of stitches that equal the width you want for the top of the neck opening, not counting steek stitches; approx 8" wide for an average adult size. For a rounded (scooped) neck, put about 5" to 6" worth of stitches on a thread and decrease away the additional 2" to 3" on either side as follows: For a wide, shallow curve, k2tog, k steek, ssk *every* round. For a deeper curve, decrease as above *every-other* round. When total wanted width is achieved, work straight to shoulder height. Knit one plain round to simplify shoulder weaving. Put all stitches on a thread.

I-Cord V-neck border; the neck shaping is worked outside the center steek; k2tog, k3, knit steek, k3, ssk.

Pullover Square Neck: How deep do you want the neck opening? How wide do you want the neck opening? What final border will you use and how much will it "fill in" the neck opening? Put full center neck-width stitches on a thread. Cast on steek. Continue straight to shoulder.

Cardigan Square Neck: The square corners will be dragged down a bit by the weight of the fabric (and the buttons) and will not hold their squareness too well. However, if you are knitting a relatively short, lightweight cardigan, proceed as for Pullover.

Now you are a knitting designer. You have chosen colors, worked a swatch, sized your garment, centered motifs, decided about sleeves, armhole depth, neck shaping, etc. Refer to the preceeding chapter for detailed techniques on all the above.

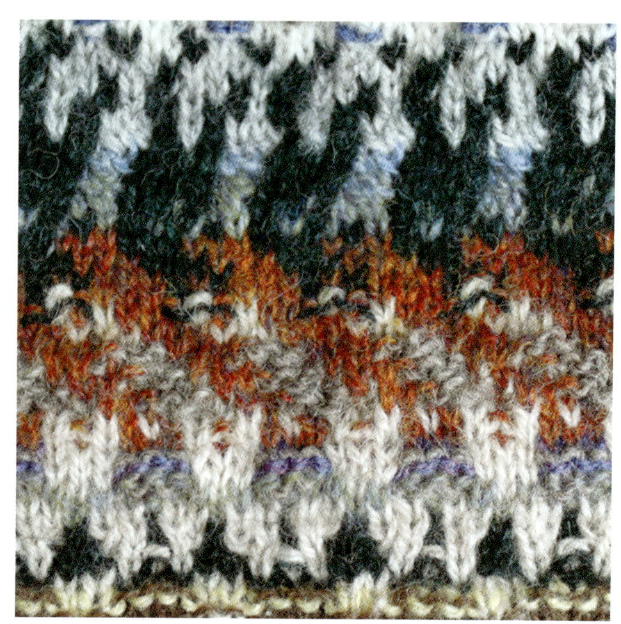

color pattern combined with texture

These two swatches follow the OXO chart on page 5, with different colorways.

Chapter 4: Miscellaneous

Small Circumferences on Two Circs

Decades ago, Joyce Williams came up with a splendid alternative to working on sets of 4 or 5 dp needles. She arranged the stitches onto two 24" circular needles and only had to change needles twice in a round instead of 3 or 4 times. Always knit with the beginning and end of the same needle, photo below.

Knitting Back-Backwards

If you wish for an alternative to purling back in color-pattern, you may knit stitches from the right needle onto the left needle as follows: insert tip of left needle into the back of the stitch on the right needle. Wrap the working wool anti-clockwise around the needle and hook it through. Slide the stitch off the right needle, which feels quite peculiar the first few hundred times. EZ called this Looking-Glass Knitting.

You are actually purling back from the front, so if the above doesn't make sense, grab your knitting and purl a few stitches. As you are doing that, peer over the top of the needles and see what is happening on the other side when you purl. Turn, and duplicate what you saw.

This is not just a parlor trick, but most useful for Entrelac, Short Rows, sock heels, Aran bobbles, etc.

Over and Under

For several years there were heated discussions at Knitting Camp about whether or not it was permissible for a knitter to switch hands in the middle of a color project.

For instance, if you hold the light color in your right hand and the dark in your left, it is common for the light color to travel over the dark across the back of your work.

If you switch hands/colors in the middle of a project, the dark will travel over the light and, frequently, there will be a noticeable difference in your knitting. Sometimes it looks like a dye-lot change; sometimes a prominent motif will become submerged.

Most knitters don't take any chances and once they have assigned a color to a hand, they never change. For other knitters, there is no difference and they switch hands/colors all the time so that the color that has the most stitches is in the fastest hand.

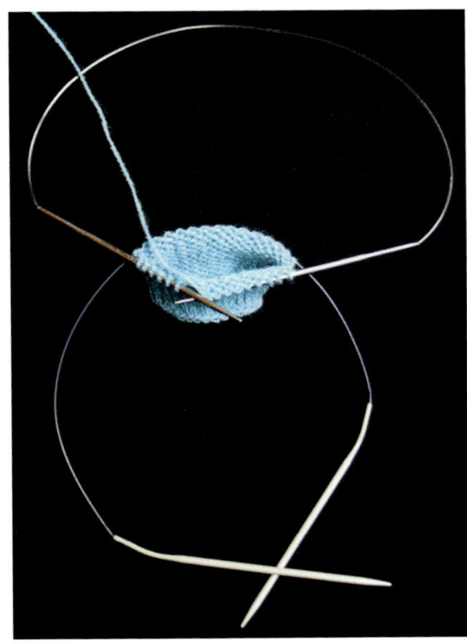

Can you see where Amy switched hands in the middle of this example?

Picture Knitting

Traditional Scandinavian and Fair Isle color-pattern motifs provide a particular "song" to each round and the repeated rhythm is most soothing and comforting to knit.

On the other hand, picture-knitting is the reverse. No two rounds are the same and it is exciting to see the images emerge from your needles. Examples in Stranded knitting are the Weeping Sun/Moon on page 41; examples in Armenian Knitting are on pages 24, 31 and the Hawk's Head, below.

Color Choices

Tone, value, shade, tint, and intensity can be intimidating terms for some of us. However, you needn't necessarily steep yourself in color theory in order to choose colors wisely.

Skeins of wool that look beautiful side-by-side on the sofa, often become muddy when combined and may result in a "tweed" effect. Colors that are too homogenous may look boring when knitted side-by-side.

Contrast is critical; too much or too little can make an outstanding design uninteresting. Our eyes and pre-conceived notions can effect our choices. A color that you are sure is a "light", may turn out to be a "medium" when compared to the other colors in your palette. Below are four methods that help you remove the color (or tint) and compare brightness within your array. This is just to help you distinguish between lights, mediums, and darks.

1. Pick up several strands from each skein and twist them together. If you can see the difference in the two colors (like a barber pole) you're ok; if the twisted bit becomes a 3rd color, experiment further.
2. Look at the colors through a telidiscope; an offending shade or a dull contrast may be more noticeable.
3. Look through a piece of "ruby lith" (found in quilt shops) to distinguish light shades from dark.
4. Put your intended choices on a copy machine or scanner, then scan using only black and white tones.

Practice Cap to Balance Motifs

If you'd like to knit a quick cap to practice Cully's Pattern Centering concept *(p49)*, here are instructions and two possible schematics that use the 24-stitch chart on page 5. The motif has a single center stitch.

To fit the 24-stitch chart into a 20" cap (@ 5 sts to 1"), with 3 seam sts at each side (diagram page 57):

A. Multiply circumference x gauge = 120.

B. Subtract the 6 seam sts from 120 (114).
C. Make the number divisible by 4 (112).
D. Add 2 sts for centers front and back (114).
E. Add seam stitches back in (120); this is the number to cast on.
F. Divide 112 by 4 to get 28 sts in each quarter.
G. Divide 28 by 24, which leaves 4 left-over sts.
H. Count 4 sts in from left edge of the chart to find your starting stitch.

Begin the round: Cast on 120. Work 3 seam sts, then begin at your starting stitch and follow the chart from R to L. Continue as described on page 49, *Centering a Color Pattern.*

Or, you can have 1 seam stitch (diagram below), either a background stitch or a Pivot point, which puts your starting stitch 5 stitches in from left edge of chart.

Then try 5, 7 or 9 seam sts at each side and maybe fill them with a different pattern altogether. Caps are quickly knitted and are wonderful for trying things out before you launch into a sweater.

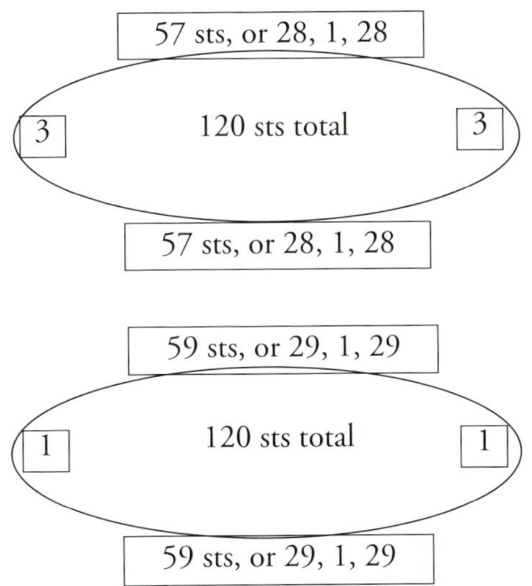

Fixing a Mistake a Few Rounds Back

Rather than ripping back a few inches of body or sleeve, you can drop off the needle only the stitches above the mistake. Rip these stitches back, one row at a time, to the error. Reknit the offending bit properly and knit up all the ladders again to the top.

This is relatively easy to do in plain or texture knitting; for instance, if you've crossed a cable in the wrong direction. However, in two-color knitting it can be a bit trickier.

Joyce Williams came up with this idea to keep track of the strands across the back: After ripping out each row, put a coilless pin over the pairs of strands from that row. Repeat for each ripped row. Then, when knitting up again, you clearly can see the strands that belong to each row.

Armenian Knitting

The origins of this knitting style remain mysterious. The technique was brought to light by Elsa Schiaparelli in Paris, 1927, through her famous Bowknot pullover.

The technique is simple enough; "trap" a second color behind the main color, even throughout many inches of solid, unpatterned knitting. Then when you want to introduce a motif, the second color is right there and ready to be knitted. Even though there may be only one relatively small motif, the entire garment is a uniform thickness.

The resulting fabric has no elasticity at all; the carried color is like a weft thread, so you must knit to size and not rely on blocking.

This idea opened up a wide panoply of possibilities for Meg and Joyce Williams. Together they designed a number of sweaters and caps and combined them in their co-authored book, *Armenian Knitting.*

outside and inside of Armenian knitting

Intarsia In the Round

This is a technique to achieve an isolated motif using neither Armenian knitting nor regular back and forth Intarsia. Mary Thomas refers to as Festive Knitting.

On this sock we wanted to continue the leg pattern down the top of the foot.

- Knit across the motif with red and grey.
- *Drop grey and continue around the foot with red.
- Knit across the arch – only the red stitches of that row; slip stitches that are to be grey.

* Twist the 2 colors around each other and knit-back-backward *(p55)* all grey stitches in that row; slip red stitches.

- Drop the grey, slip all motif stitches to R needle.
- Pick up red and work around foot.
- Ahhhh, the grey is waiting for you – knit across motif with both colors.
- Repeat from *.

The sweater below has a yoke pattern that begins with an isolated motif of Intarsia in the round.

EZ's After-Thought Pockets

Indeed, you can install EZ's After-Thought Pockets in an all-over patterned garment.

If you have 2 colors in the row, snip half a stitch of one color in the middle of the proposed pocket, and ravel in each direction for a narrow opening. If too wide, the top edge will stretch and sag; make it just wide enough to admit your hand. Snip half a stitch of the second color and ravel to the same points.

Pick up the lower stitches and work border of your choice (hem, Garter stitch, I-Cord, etc). Pick up the obvious sts in the upper row and twist-and-pick-up stranded loops between the sts so you have the same number of stitches on top and bottom.

Work back and forth across the top in solid pocket color. Keep 3 edge stitches in Garter stitch (so it will lie flat when sewing down) and the center section in Stocking stitch. Inc at each edge to widen the pocket as you knit to wanted depth.

Cast off and sew pocket down on 3 sides *(photo p59)*.

Intarsia in the round worked for first half of the center diamond. Begin with the third row of the pattern and work the first 2 rows later, in duplicate stitch.

EZ's After-Thought Pockets on an interlocking color pattern. Note p-w-y-c *(p17) on both lower edge and cardigan border and EZ's Hidden I-Cord buttonholes (p38).*

Jogless Jog

Circular knitting spirals like a barber pole; the end does not meet the beginning. Many all-over color patterned garments are knitted at a relatively small gauge, making the circular-jog-factor practically irrelevant for all but the fussiest knitter.

For cardigans, begin in the middle of the center-front steek, and pay no attention to the jog. For pullovers, begin the new round at a side "seam".

Solid Stripes: The jog visible in a horizontal solid stripe of 2 or more rounds is the worst offender; you can see it from across the room. A jog can be eliminated as follows: At the end of the first round of the new color, with the tip of the right needle, lift the righthand side of the stitch in the row below the first stitch of the round (it is a contrasting color). Put it on the left needle and K2tog which shifts the first stitch one to the left. Knit on. Before beginning the next motif above the stripe, you may shift back to the original "first" stitch.

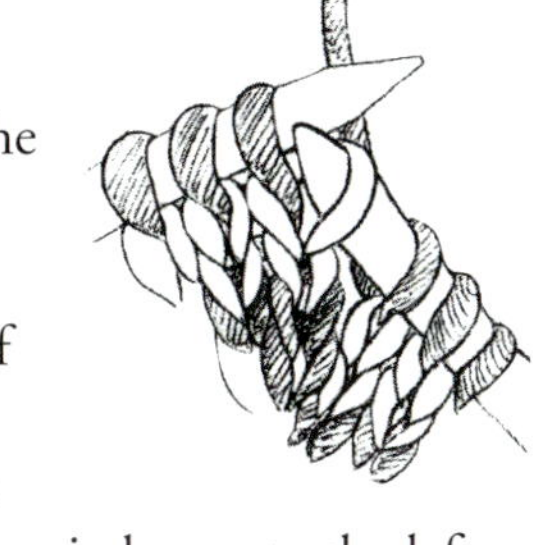

To obviate the jog in the midst of an all-over motif, with separated patterns (like an OXO), see box at right.

Inside and outside of an After-Thought pocket; notice the narrow opening, widening pocket and 3 Garter stitches along each edge.

For an interlocking pattern, use *Jogless Darning-In* described on page 20.

The Shaded Leaf *sweater below, designed and knitted by Elizabeth Zimmermann in 1959, is a good example of how to defeat the jog in circular color-pattern knitting.*

The jog is most visible when the first stitch of the new round travels through a motif – so don't let it.

Simply re-assign the first stitch to keep it from being within the leaf; the dotted line shows how the first stitch travels to the left when a new leaf begins.

Complete the last leaf of the round; yes, it goes past the starting stitch. Then move up to the next chart line.

When the second vertical leaf is finished and there is a more-or-less plain round, you can return to the original first stitch and repeat the evasion.

When travelling to the left, you will have an extra back-ground stitch separating the first and last leaf. If you are finicky, you can decrease 1 when you begin to shift to the left (this was not done here) and increase 1 when you go back to the original first stitch.

You might choose to shift to the right - in which case, work a sneaky single increase when the shift begins; then decrease one stitch as you return to the original beginning stitch.

Latvian Braid

This clever and decorative technique appears frequently around the cuffs of traditional Latvian Mittens and is worked as follows:

With 2 contrasting colors (A and B), work a set-up round of (k1A, k1B) alternately around.

Now, bring both wools to the front and...

1. (P1A, p1B) alternately, and always bring the next color ***over*** the old. Yes, the wools will become quite tangled, but persevere to the end of the round.

2. (P1A, p1B) as before, but this time bring each next color ***under*** the old and watch the tangle resolve itself and the chevron lean in the opposite direction. A tip to remember in which direction the chevron will lean: Left-Over; Right-Under.

When applying this to the circumference of a sweater, it occurred to Meg to change directions at each quarter point around the body. This shortens the length of tangle and produces a pretty mirror-image at each turn; see centers of the braids in the photos below for examples of this. Try only one round (either *over* or *under*) for a handsome half-chevron.

Centering Motifs for Yoke Sweaters

Cully has applied his centering formula *(p49)* to yoke sweaters as well.

Pullover: The motif repeat must fit evenly into the stitches on the needle; increase or decrease a few stitches to achieve this. Generally speaking, yoke patterns are rather small, so the change in your stitch count should be minimal.

Begin at center front and count back in increments of the pattern repeat until you are behind the left shoulder – somewhere between 1/4 and 1/2 of the stitches on the needle. End after counting a full motif repeat and begin the round at that point.

Cardigan (or Sleeves): The motif need not fit into the stitches on the needle. If your motif has a single center stitch *(chart p49)*, make your stitch count odd (do not include steek or underarm stitches). Count from the center-back (or sleeve top) stitch in increments of the pattern repeat until you reach the steek (or underarm). The last stitch will be somewhere within your motif - begin on that stitch.

If your motif has two center stitches, make the stitch count even. Count from one of the two center back (or sleeve top) stitches in increments of the pattern repeat until you reach the steek (or undrearm). The last stitch will be somewhere within your motif - begin on that stitch.

Amy signs her work on a shoulder saddle.

Index

fterthought pockets	see *pockets*	
ames, Kevin	variation on EZ's one-row buttonhole	38
pplied I-Cord border	see *I-Cord*	
rmenian Knitting	defined	57
rmholes	borders for vest	34
	Kangaroo Pouch	25
	knitting up around	32
	shaping for vest	52
	shaping of	25
Bajus, Janine	short row shoulder shaping	29
	tip for starting crocheted steek	30
balancing color patterns	see *patterns, centering*	
Barrington, Dee	tip on smoothing out ssk	23
binding off	3-Needle and 3-Needle I-Cord	39
blips	see *purl blips*	
blocking tips		41
borders, applied	see *I-Cord*	
borders, armhole	see *Armholes*	
borders, cardigan	after finishing body	35
	ratio of sts to rows	32
	using purl-when-you-can	17
borders, lower	Checkerboard Garter stitch	17
	Checkerboard ribbing	17
	choosing	16
	Corrugated ribbing	16
	curling	13
	hems	17,18
	just start knitting	19
	Purl-when-You-Can (PWYC)	17
borders, neck	for cardigans	36
	for pullovers	35
braid, Latvian	how to	60
Brunette, Cheryl	More-or-Less Right Formula	19
buttonholes	EZ's Hidden I-Cord	38
	EZ's Looped I-Cord	38
	EZ's One-Row	38
	in Corrugated Ribbing	37
	spacing of	37
caps	centering practice	56,57
	swatch	8
	technique practice	6
casting off	see *binding off*	
casting on	Cable	14
	German twisted variation	13
	long -tail	13
	provisional crocheted	14
CDD	see *decreasing*	
centered dbl decrease	see *decreasing*	
centering color patterns	see *patterns, centering*	
charts	how to read	5
Checkerboard ribbing	see *borders, lower*	
circular knitting	see *establishing circular knitting*	
color choices		56
Corrugated rib	see *borders, lower*	
crocheted cast-on	see *cast on, provisional crocheted*	
crocheted steeks	see *steeks*	
curling lower border	see *borders, lower*	
darning in ends	see *jogless darning in*	
decreasing	centered double decrease (CDD)	24
	in color pattern	23
	k2tog	23
	keeping track of (string thing)	32
	shaping sleeves with CDD	33
	spacing evenly (More-or-Less Formula)	19
	ssk	23
designing your own		42
ease	recommended amount	43
ends	see *jogless darning in*	
EPS	defined	43
	for drop-shoulder	45,46
	for seamless yoke	44,45
establishing circular knitting		15,16
EZ's Applied I-Cord Border	see *I-Cord*	
EZ's One-Row buttonhole	see *buttonholes*	
Fair Isle	definition	4
Festive Knitting	see *intarsia in the round*	
fixing a mistake	in previous rounds	57
gauge	importance of	10,11,42
	measuring accurately	8
	using gauge to change size of garment	12
Glover, Medrith	buttonhole for corrugated ribbing	37
grafting	aka Kitchener or weaving	40
	in 2 colors	41
gusset		52
half gusset	see *gusset*	
Hall, Mary	trick for last st of Cable cast on	14
hems	see *borders, lower*	
holding yarns	which hand(s) to use	6,7
I-Cord	applied border	35
	buttonholes	38
increasing	in color pattern	21,22
	keeping track of (string thing)	32
	knit into back of stitch of row below	22
	lifted	21
	M1 (make one)	21
	spacing evenly (More-or-Less Formula)	19
intarsia in the round	how to	58
jogless darning in	how to	20
jogs in color pattern	avoiding with Jogless Jog	59
joining	sleeves to body	34
joining circular knitting	being careful not to twist	16
joining new colors		6,19
	using spit splice	20
just start knitting	see *borders, lower*	

kangaroo pouch	see *armholes*	
Kitchener stitch	see *grafting*	
knitting back backwards	how to	55
	when working short rows	27
knitting, circular	see *establishing circular knitting*	
knit-up stitches	around armhole	32
	flanking a steek	15
	in color pattern	32
	ratio of rows to stitches	32
Latvian braid	see *braid, Latvian*	
Long-tail cast on	see *casting on*	
looking glass knitting	see *knitting back backwards*	
lower borders	see *borders, lower*	
McGregor, Sheila	steeking technique	31
mirror imaging	color pattern (using Pivot stitch)	47
	color pattern on yoke sweater	60
	increases	21,22
mistakes	see *fixing a mistake*	
More-or-Less right	spacing formula	19
neck shaping	see *shaping*	
needles	using 2 for small circumferences	55
Norwegian method	see *steeks*	
over and under	see *stranded knitting*	
OXOs	definition	4
patterns, centering	formula for	49
	in yoke sweaters	60
	using Pivot sts	47
Pearson, Michael	steeking technique	31
peeries	definition	4
pick up ratio	see *ratio*	
picture knitting		56
pivot stitches		47,48
pockets	afterthought	58
practice cap	see *caps*	
provisonal cast on	see *casting on*	
purl blips	hiding in Corrugated rib	16
	in purl-when-you-can borders	17
purl-when-you-can	see *borders, lower* and *borders, cardigan*	
ratio	of rows to stitches	32
reading charts	see *charts*	
resizing garments	by adding stitches	12
	by changing gauge	12
	see *EPS*	43
ribbing	see *borders, lower*	
Robinson, Nancy	eliminating knot in cast on	14
	row gauge experiment	11
row gauge	see *gauge*	
Rowe, Mary	buttonhole formula	37
rows to stitches ratio	see *ratio*	
Scandinavian method	see *steeks*	
sewing machine	see *steeks*	
shaping	armholes for vests	52
	body	27,51
	down sleeve top	32
	neck	26,53
	shoulders using short rows	29
Short Rows	for body shaping	27
	for shoulder shaping	2
	Japanese method (using pin)	2
	wrap and turn (w&t) method	2
	yo method	2
sleeves	from the bottom up	33,3
	from the top down	3
	on two 24-inch circular needles	5
	shaping down sleeve top	3
solid color rounds	in color knitting	2
spacing	see *buttonholes*	
	see *increases or decreases*	
speed bump	use of	6,
	how to	3
speed swatch	see *swatch*	
spit splicing	see *joining new colors*	
steam block		4
steeks	cardigan	30,3
	cutting	3
	Norwegian method	3
	planning	15,30,42
	Scandinavian method	31
	securing with crochet	30
	securing with sewing machine	31
	wrapped	18
stitch gauge	see *gauge*	
stitches to rows ratio	see *ratio*	
stranded knitting	trapping	9
	long floats across the back	9
	over and under	55
string thing	making & using	32
Swansen, Cully	centering color patterns (formula)	49
swatch cap	see *swatch*	8
swatch	cap	8
	speed	12
sweaters	EPS yoke pullover	44
	EPS modified drop shoulder	45
	EPS straight drop shoulder	46
trapping	see *stranded knitting*	
using Pivot stitches	see *pivot stitches*	
waist shaping	see *shaping, body*	51
Walker, Barbara G	wrap and turn for short rows	27
washing tips		41
weaving	see *grafting*	
Williams, Joyce	alternate method of trapping	9
	shoulder shaping using short rows	29
	trick for fixing mistakes in two colors	57
wrapped steek	see *steeks*	
yoke sweaters	EPS yoke pullover	44
	centering color patterns (formula)	60
Zimmermann, Elizabeth	applied I-Cord borders	35
	EPS (Elizabeth's Percentage System)	43
	EZ's Hidden I-Cord Buttonhole	38
	EZ's Looped I-Cord Buttonhole	38
	EZ's One-Row buttonhole	38
	kangaroo pouch for armhole shaping	25
	knotless beginning for casting on	13
	ratio of stitches to rows	22

page	name of item	designer	pattern
6 and 7	Practice Cap	Meg Swansen	p6
8 left	Rosemarkie Waistcoat	Alice Starmore*	CC
8 right	Norwegian Sleeve Cardigan	Meg Swansen	n/a
10 left	Kitties Cardigan	Meg Swansen	n/a
10 right	Celtic Swirl	Meg Swansen	SPP35
11 right	Fair Isle Pillow	Meg Swansen	SPP32
11 left	Springtime in Wisconsin	Meg Swansen	MSK
12 right	Oregon, different colors	Alice Starmore*	SC
15 left	Rosemarkie Waistcoat	Alice Starmore*	CC
15 right	Norwegian Rose	Meg Swansen	SPP34
16 left	(unpublished)	Amy Detjen	n/a
16 right	Faux Fair Isle	Amy Detjen	SFC
17 left	Oregon, different colors	Alice Starmore*	SC
17 right	Latvian Mitten Cardigan	Meg Swansen	SPP33
18 top	Shaded Aspen Leaf	Elizabeth Z	EZKW
19 left	3-In-1 Sweater	Elizabeth Z	KAR
19 right	Gordian Knot Pullover	Meg Swansen	SPP31
20 left	Turkish Maple	Meg Swansen	SPP21
20 right	Cully's Vest	Elizabeth Z	EZKW
21 left	Halland Jersey	Meg Swansen	n/a
21 right	Coastal Jersey	Meg Swansen	n/a
22 left	Arch-Shaped Stockings	Meg Swansen	SPP2
22 right	Latvian Mitten Cardigan	Meg Swansen	SPP33
23 left	Faroe Vest	Elizabeth Z	SFC
23 right	Fair Isle Vest	Meg Swansen	DVD
24 up R	Shaded Aspen Leaf	Elizabeth Z	EZKW
24 left	Butterfly Vest	Meg Swansen	AK
24 low R	Dancing Crones Sweater	Meg Swansen	WG83
25 up L	Dalmore	Alice Starmore*	CC
24 low L	Turkish Maple	Meg Swansen	SPP21
25 right	Fair Isle Vest	Meg Swansen	DVD
26-1	Columbine	Kevin Ames	SFC
26-2	Delsbo Cardigan	Meg Swansen	SPP14
26-3	Circles	Joyce Williams	LD
26-4	Christmas Past	Dale Long	SPP8
26-5	Turkish Maple	Meg Swansen	SPP21
29 up L	Butterfly Vest	Meg Swansen	AK
29 low L	Woodland Vest	Janine Bajus	n/a
29 up R	Acorn sweater	Janine Bajus	n/a
29 low R	Acorn Sweater	Janine Bajus	n/a
31	Flower Vest	Meg Swansen	AK
32 left	Cuff-to-Cuff	Meg Swansen	SO47
32 right	Russian Prime	Meg Swansen	MSK/DVD
33 left	Norwegian Rose	Meg Swansen	SPP34
33 center	Latvian Mitten Cardigan	Meg Swansen	SPP33
32 right	Cuff-to-Cuff	Meg Swansen	SO47
34 top L	Cardigan Details	Meg Swansen	MSK/DVD
34 low L	Cossack Vest	Meg Swansen	AK
34 low R	Autumn Color Cardigan	Betts Lampers*	SFC
35 left	Sacred Trees	Ron Schweitzer	SPP23
35 right	Celtic Pillow	Meg Swansen	SPP32

page	name of item	designer	pattern
36 up R	Welcome Back Sun	Marilyn van Keppel	SPP22
36 left	Aspen Yoke sweaters	Meg Swansen	SPP20
36 right	Faux Fair Isle	Amy Detjen	SFC
37 left	Two Yoke Sweaters	EZ/MS	SPP4
37 right	Oregon, different colors	Alice Starmore*	SC
38 left	Shirt Tail Fair Isle	Ann Feitelson	SPP29
38 right	Turkish Coat	Meg Swansen	n/a
39 L & R	swatches for EZ's NL#1	Joyce Williams	OK
40 left	Autumn Color Cardigan	Betts Lampers*	SFC/SPP30
40 right	Fair Isle Vest	Meg Swansen	DVD
41	Weeping Sun/Moon	Meg Swansen	SPP18
42 left	Square Rigged Vest	Meg Swansen	n/a
42 right	Delsbo Cardigan	Meg Swansen	SPP14
44 left	unknown, from collection of	Elizabeth Z	n/a
44 right	Henley Yoke Pullover	Meg Swansen	SO3
45 right	Two Yoke Sweaters	EZ/MS	SPP 4
46 (1)	Latvian Mitten Cardigan	Meg Swansen	SPP33
46 (2)	Cuff-to-Cuff	Meg Swansen	SO47
46 (3)	Cuff-to-Cuff	Meg Swansen	SO47
46 (4)	Russian Prime	Meg Swansen	MSK/DVD
48 (1)	RedFair Isle	Meg Swansen	n/a
48 (2)	Turkish Pullover	Meg Swansen	n/a
48 (3)	Norwegian Rose	Meg Swansen	SPP34
48 (4)	Russian Prime	Meg Swansen	MSK/DVD
52 left	Autumn Color Cardigan	Betts Lampers	SFC
52 right	Bohus Yoke from collection of	Meg Swansen	n/a
53 left	Faroe Vest	Elizabeth Z	SFC
53 right	Mimbres Vest	Meg Swansen	DVD
54 up R	unknown, from collection of	Elizabeth Z	n/a
54 left	Fair Isle Vestblue/green	Meg Swansen	n/a
54 low R	Fair Isle Vest-red	Meg Swansen	n/a
56 left	Hawk's Head	Meg Swansen	n/a
56 up R	Cuff-to-Cuff	Meg Swansen	SO47
56 low R	Fair Isle Vest	Meg Swansen	DVD
57 right	(One of) Three Hats	Meg Swansen	AK
58 up L	Arch-Shaped Stocking	Meg Swansen	SPP2
58 low L	Cuff-to-Cuff	Meg Swansen	SO47
58 low R	Kitties Cardigan	Meg Swansen	n/a
59 left	Turkish Coat	Meg Swansen	n/a
59 right	Aspen Leaf Pullover	Elizabeth Z	EZKW
60 up L	Men's pullover	Meg Swansen	n/a
60 low L	Scribble Sweater	Meg Swansen	WG71
60 low R	Abalone	Alice Starmore*	PCH

*knitted by Amy Detjen, n/a = not available

Books & Patterns: AK =*Armenian Knitting*, **CC** =*Celtic Collection*, **DVD** = *separate dvd for each design*, **EZKW** =*Knitting Workshop*, **LD** =*Latvian Dreams*, **MSK** =*Meg Swansen's Knitting*, **OK** =*The Opinionated Knitter*, **PCH** =*Pacific Coast Highway*, **SC** =*Scottish Collection*, **SFC** =*Sweaters from Camp*, **SO** =*Spun Out*, **SPP** =*Schoolhouse Press Pattern*, **WG** =*Wool Gathering*

SPPs (Schoolhouse Press Patterns)

SPP#1: EZ's Butterfly Vest
SPP#2. Arch-Shaped Stockings*
SPP#3. Box-the-Compass
SPP#4. EZ and MS Yoke-patterned pullover & cardigan*
SPP#5. ABCSJ (Adult, Baby, Child's Surprise Jacket)
SPP#6. Sock-Within-a-Sock (double-knit), Beverly Royce
SPP#7. Near Solstice Lace Shawl, Bridget Rorem
SPP#8. Christmas Past Shetland Pullover*, Dale Long
SPP#9. Lace Alphabet Scarf, Bridget Rorem
SPP#10. Eli's Christmas Stocking*
SPP#11. Seven Hats
SPP#12. Fringed Latvian Mittens*, Lizbeth Upitis
SPP#13. EZ's Green Sweater, Sunday Holm
SPP#14. Swedish Delsbo Jacket*
SPP#15. Elizabeth's & Meg's Two Guernseys
SPP#16. Flowers of Life*, Ron Schweitzer
SPP#17. Cully's Cabled Yoke sweater & Cap
SPP#18. Weeping Sun & Moon*
SPP#19. The Tomten
SPP#20. Aspen Yoke pullover*
SPP#21. Turkish Maple* *and* Turkish Ocean*
SPP#22. *Welcome Back Sun* Cardigan*, Marilyn van Keppel
SPP#23. Sacred Trees*, Ron Schweitzer
SPP#24. 3-Cornered Lace Icelandic Neck Scarf & Shawl, Marilyn van Keppel
SPP#25. If I Could Fly Froese Shawl, Bridget Rorem
SPP#26. EZ's Doll Clothes (for 16-1/2" doll)
SPP#27. Pansy Triangle Lace shawl, Amy Detjen
SPP#28. Ritual Dance*, Ron Schweitzer
SPP#29. Snow Sky*, Ann Swanson *(from SFC)*
SPP#30. Shirt Tail Fair Isle Pullover*, Ann Feitelson *(from SFC)*
SPP#31. Autumn Color Card igan*, Betts Lampers *(from SFC)*
SPP#32. Gordian Knot Pullover* *(from SFC)*
SPP#33. Fair Isle/Celtic Pillows*
SPP#34. Giant Latvian Mitten Cardigan*
SPP#35. Norwegian Rose Cardigan*
SPP#36. Celtic Swirl*
SPP#37. Twisted Stitch Peplum Jacket

* = color pattern
SFC -= Sweaters From Camp
photos and descriptions at **schoolhousepress.com**

DVDs from Schoolhouse Press
The *Knitting Glossary* contains over 130 techniques

Saddle Sleeve Jacket and Twisted Stitch Hat, MS
Round the Bend Jacket and Puzzle Pillow, MS
Elizabeth Zimmermann's Ribwarmer, MS
A Shawl Collared Vest, MS
Knitting Around, EZ & MS
Knitting Lace, MS
The Russian Prime*, MS
Guernsey Pullover, MS
Elizabeth Zimmermann's Baby Surprise Jacket, MS
A Fair Isle Vest*, MS
Knitting Glossary, EZ & MS
Knitting Workshop with Elizabeth Zimmerman
Spiral Yoke, MS
Mimbres Vest*, MS
Cardigan Details*, MS
Swedish Dubbelmössa* and Scarf, MS

* = color pattern
EZ = Elizabeth Zimmermann
MS = Meg Swansen
photos and descriptions at **schoolhousepress.com**